1B

FOUR CORNERS

Second Edition

Student's Book
with Digital Pack

JACK C. RICHARDS & DAVID BOHLKE

CAMBRIDGE

Shaftesbury Road, Cambridge CB2 8EA, United Kingdom

One Liberty Plaza, 20th Floor, New York, NY 10006, USA

477 Williamstown Road, Port Melbourne, VIC 3207, Australia

314–321, 3rd Floor, Plot 3, Splendor Forum, Jasola District Centre, New Delhi – 110025, India

103 Penang Road, #05–06/07, Visioncrest Commercial, Singapore 238467

Cambridge University Press & Assessment is a department of the University of Cambridge.

We share the University's mission to contribute to society through the pursuit of education, learning and research at the highest international levels of excellence.

www.cambridge.org
Information on this title: www.cambridge.org/9781009285988

© Cambridge University Press & Assessment 2012, 2019, 2023

First published 2012
Second edition 2019

20 19 18 17 16 15 14 13

Printed in Poland by Opolgraf

A catalogue record for this publication is available from the British Library

ISBN 978-1-009-28597-1   Student's Book with Digital Pack 1
ISBN 978-1-009-28610-7   Student's Book with Digital Pack 1A
ISBN 978-1-009-28598-8   Student's Book with Digital Pack 1B
ISBN 978-1-108-63367-3   Teacher's Edition with Complete Assessment Program 1
ISBN 978-1-009-28599-5   Full Contact with Digital Pack 1
ISBN 978-1-009-28600-8   Full Contact with Digital Pack 1A
ISBN 978-1-009-28616-9   Full Contact with Digital Pack 1B
ISBN 978-1-009-28593-3   Presentation Plus Level 1

Additional resources for this publication at www.cambridge.org/fourcorners

Cambridge University Press & Assessment has no responsibility for the persistence or accuracy of URLs for external or third-party internet websites referred to in this publication and does not guarantee that any content on such websites is, or will remain, accurate or appropriate.

Authors' acknowledgments

Many people contributed to the development of *Four Corners*. The authors and publisher would like to particularly thank the following **reviewers**:

Nele Noe, **Academy for Educational Development, Qatar Independent Secondary School for Girls**, Doha, Qatar; Pablo Stucchi, **Antonio Raimondi School** and **Instituto San Ignacio de Loyola**, Lima, Peru; Nadeen Katz, **Asia University**, Tokyo, Japan; Tim Vandenhoek, **Asia University**, Tokyo, Japan; Celso Frade and Sonia Maria Baccari de Godoy, **Associação Alumni**, São Paulo, Brazil; Rosane Bandeira, **Atlanta Idiomas**, Manaus, Brazil; Cacilda Reis da Silva, **Atlanta Idiomas**, Manaus, Brazil; Gretta Sicsu, **Atlanta Idiomas**, Manaus, Brazil; Naila Maria Cañiso Ferreira, **Atlanta Idiomas**, Manaus, Brazil; Hothnã Moraes de Souza Neto, **Atlanta Idiomas**, Manaus, Brazil; Jacqueline Kurtzious, **Atlanta Idiomas**, Manaus, Brazil; José Menezes Ribeiro Neto, **Atlanta Idiomas**, Manaus, Brazil; Sheila Ribeiro Cordeiro, **Atlanta Idiomas**, Manaus, Brazil; Juliana Fernandes, **Atlanta Idiomas**, Manaus, Brazil; Aline Alexandrina da Silva, **Atlanta Idiomas**, Manaus, Brazil; Kari Miller, **Binational Center**, Quito, Ecuador; Alex K. Oliveira, **Boston University**, Boston, MA, USA; Noriko Furuya, **Bunka Gakuen University**, Tokyo, Japan; Robert Hickling, **Bunka Gakuen University**, Tokyo, Japan; John D. Owen, **Bunka Gakuen University**, Tokyo, Japan; Elisabeth Blom, **Casa Thomas Jefferson**, Brasília, Brazil; Lucilena Oliveira Andrade, **Centro Cultural Brasil Estados Unidos (CCBEU Belém)**, Belém, Brazil; Marcelo Franco Borges, **Centro Cultural Brasil Estados Unidos (CCBEU Belém)**, Belém, Brazil; Geysa de Azevedo Moreira, **Centro Cultural Brasil Estados Unidos (CCBEU Belém)**, Belém, Brazil; Anderson Felipe Barbosa Negrão, **Centro Cultural Brasil Estados Unidos (CCBEU Belém)**, Belém, Brazil; Henry Grant, **CCBEU – Campinas**, Campinas, Brazil; Maria do Rosário, **CCBEU – Franca**, Franca, Brazil; Ane Cibele Palma, **CCBEU Inter Americano**, Curitiba, Brazil; Elen Flavia Penques da Costa, **Centro de Cultura Idiomas – Taubaté**, Taubaté, Brazil; Inara Lúcia Castillo Couto, **CEL LEP – São Paulo**, São Paulo, Brazil; Sonia Patricia Cardoso, **Centro de Idiomas Universidad Manuela Beltrán**, Barrio Cedritos, Colombia; Geraldine Itiago Losada, **Centro Universitario Grupo Sol (Musali)**, Mexico City, Mexico; Nick Hilmers, **DePaul University**, Chicago, IL, USA; Monica L. Montemayor Menchaca, **EDIMSA**, Metepec, Mexico; Angela Whitby, **Edu-Idiomas Language School**, Cholula, Puebla, Mexico; Mary Segovia, **El Monte Rosemead Adult School**, Rosemead, CA, USA; Dr. Deborah Aldred, **ELS Language Centers, Middle East Region**, Abu Dhabi, United Arab Emirates; Leslie Lott, **Embassy CES**, Ft. Lauderdale, FL, USA; M. Martha Lengeling, **Escuela de Idiomas**, Guanajuato, Mexico; Pablo Frias, **Escuela de Idiomas UNAPEC**, Santo Domingo, Dominican Republic; Tracy Vanderhoek, **ESL Language Center**, Toronto, Canada; Kris Vicca and Michael McCollister, **Feng Chia University**, Taichung, Taiwan; Flávia Patricia do Nascimento Martins, **First Idiomas**, Sorocaba, Brazil; Andrea Taylor, **Florida State University in Panama**, Panamá, Panama; Carlos Lizárraga González, **Grupo Educativo Angloamericano**, Mexico City, Mexico; Bo-Kyung Lee, **Hankuk University of Foreign Studies**, Seoul, South Korea; Dr. Martin Endley, **Hanyang University**, Seoul, South Korea; Mauro Luiz Pinheiro, **IBEU Ceará**, Ceará, Brazil; Ana Lúcia da Costa Maia de Almeida, **IBEU Copacabana**, Copacabana, Brazil; Maristela Silva, **ICBEU Manaus**, Manaus, Brazil; Magaly Mendes Lemos, **ICBEU São José dos Campos**, São José dos Campos, Brazil; Augusto Pelligrini Filho, **ICBEU São Luis**, São Luis, Brazil; Leonardo Mercado, **ICPNA**, Lima, Peru; Lucia Rangel Lugo, **Instituto Tecnológico de San Luis Potosí**, San Luis Potosí, Mexico; Maria Guadalupe Hernández Lozada, **Instituto Tecnológico de Tlalnepantla**, Tlalnepantla de Baz, Mexico; Karen Stewart, **International House Veracruz**, Veracruz, Mexico; Tom David, **Japan College of Foreign Languages**, Tokyo, Japan; Andy Burki, **Korea University, International Foreign Language School**, Seoul, South Korea; Jinseo Noh, **Kwangwoon University**, Seoul, South Korea; Neil Donachey, **La Salle Junior and Senior High School**, Kagoshima, Japan; Rich Hollingworth, **La Salle Junior and Senior High School**, Kagoshima, Japan; Quentin Kum, **La Salle Junior and Senior High School**, Kagoshima, Japan; Geoff Oliver, **La Salle Junior and Senior High School**, Kagoshima, Japan; Martin Williams, **La Salle Junior and Senior High School**, Kagoshima, Japan; Nadezhda Nazarenko, **Lone Star College**, Houston, TX, USA; Carolyn Ho, **Lone Star College-Cy-Fair**, Cypress, TX, USA; Kaoru Kuwajima, **Meijo University**, Nagoya, Japan; Alice Ya-fen Chou, **National Taiwan University of Science and Technology**, Taipei, Taiwan; Raymond Dreyer, **Northern Essex Community College**, Lawrence, MA, USA; Mary Keter Terzian Megale, **One Way Línguas-Suzano**, São Paulo, Brazil; B. Greg Dunne, **Osaka Shoin Women's University**, Higashi-Osaka, Japan; Robert Maran, **Osaka Shoin Women's University**, Higashi-Osaka, Japan; Bonnie Cheeseman, **Pasadena Community College** and **UCLA American Language Center**, Los Angeles, CA, USA; Simon Banha, **Phil Young's English School**, Curitiba, Brazil; Oh Jun Il, **Pukyong National University**, Busan, South Korea; Carmen Gehrke, **Quatrum English Schools**, Porto Alegre, Brazil; John Duplice, **Rikkyo University**, Tokyo, Japan; Wilzania da Silva Nascimento, **Senac**, Manaus, Brazil; Miva Silva Kingston, **Senac**, Manaus, Brazil; Lais Lima, **Senac**, Manaus, Brazil; Mengjiao Wu, **Shanghai Maritime University**, Shanghai, China; Wen hsiang Su, **Shih Chien University Kaohsiung Campus**, Kaohsiung, Taiwan; Yuan-hsun Chuang, **Soo Chow University**, Taipei, Taiwan; Lynne Kim, **Sun Moon University (Institute for Language Education)**, Cheon An City, Chung Nam, South Korea; Regina Ramalho, **Talken English School**, Curitiba, Brazil; Tatiana Mendonça, **Talken English School**, Curitiba, Brazil; Ricardo Todeschini, **Talken English School**, Curitiba, Brazil; Monica Carvalho da Rocha, **Talken English School**, Joinville, Brazil; Karina Schoene, **Talken English School**, Joinville, Brazil; Diaña Peña Munoz and Zira Kuri, **The Anglo**, Mexico City, Mexico; Christopher Modell, **Tokai University**, Tokyo, Japan; Song-won Kim, **TTI (Teacher's Training Institute)**, Seoul, South Korea; Nancy Alarcón, **UNAM FES Zaragoza Language Center**, Mexico City, Mexico; Laura Emilia Fierro López, **Universidad Autónoma de Baja California**, Mexicali, Mexico; María del Rocío Domínguez Gaona, **Universidad Autónoma de Baja California**, Tijuana, Mexico; Saul Santos Garcia, **Universidad Autónoma de Nayarit**, Nayarit, Mexico; Christian Meléndez, **Universidad Católica de El Salvador**, San Salvador, El Salvador; Irasema Mora Pablo, **Universidad de Guanajuato**, Guanajuato, Mexico; Alberto Peto, **Universidad de Oaxaca**, Tehuantepec, Mexico; Carolina Rodriguez Beltan, **Universidad Manuela Beltrán, Centro Colombo Americano**, and **Universidad Jorge Tadeo Lozano**, Bogotá, Colombia; Nidia Milena Molina Rodriguez, **Universidad Manuela Beltrán** and **Universidad Militar Nueva Granada**, Bogotá, Colombia; Yolima Perez Arias, **Universidad Nacional de Colombia**, Bogotá, Colombia; Héctor Vázquez García, **Universidad Nacional Autónoma de Mexico**, Mexico City, Mexico; Pilar Barrera, **Universidad Técnica de Ambato**, Ambato, Ecuador; Deborah Hulston, **University of Regina**, Regina, Canada; Rebecca J. Shelton, **Valparaiso University, Interlink Language Center**, Valparaiso, IN, USA; Tae Lee, **Yonsei University**, Seodaemun-gu, Seoul, South Korea; Claudia Thereza Nascimento Mendes, **York Language Institute**, Rio de Janeiro, Brazil; Jamila Jenny Hakam, **ELT Consultant**, Muscat, Oman; Stephanie Smith, **ELT Consultant**, Austin, TX, USA.

Scope and sequence

LEVEL 1	Learning outcomes	Grammar	Vocabulary
Unit 7 Pages 65–74			
Food A *Breakfast, lunch, and dinner* B *I like Chinese food!* C *Meals* D *Favorite food*	**Students can …** ☑ say what meals they eat ☑ say what they like and dislike ☑ talk about their eating habits ☑ talk about their favorite food	Count and noncount nouns *Some* and *any* *How often* Time expressions	Food More food
Unit 8 Pages 75–84			
In the neighborhood A *Around town* B *How do I get to … ?* C *Fun in the city* D *A great place to visit*	**Students can …** ☑ give the locations of neighborhood places ☑ ask for and give directions ☑ talk about interesting places in their towns ☑ give a presentation on a city attraction	Prepositions of location *There is, there are*	Places in the neighborhood Places to visit
Unit 9 Pages 85–94			

What are you doing?
A *I'm looking for you.*
B *I can't talk right now.*
 	
C *These days*
D *What's new?*
	Students can …
	☑ describe what people are doing right now
	☑ ask if someone can talk right now
	☑ explain why they can't talk on the telephone
	☑ describe what people are doing these days
	☑ discuss what people are doing
		Present continuous
		  statements
		Present continuous
		  questions
			Actions and
			  prepositions
			Activities

Unit 10 Pages 95–104			
Past experiences A *Last weekend* B *You're kidding!* C *Did you make dinner last night?* D *I saw a great movie.*	**Students can …** ☑ say what they did last weekend ☑ show that they're listening ☑ express surprise ☑ talk about routine events in the past ☑ talk about past activities	Simple past regular verbs Simple past irregular verbs *Yes / no* questions	Weekend activities Things to do
Unit 11 Pages 105–114			
Getting away A *Where were you?* B *That's great!* C *My vacation* D *Travel experiences*	**Students can …** ☑ describe where they were in the past ☑ react to news ☑ talk about their last vacation ☑ describe a vacation	Past of *be* Simple past *Wh-* questions	Adjectives Vacation activities
Unit 12 Pages 115–124			
Time to celebrate A *I'm going to get married.* B *Sure. I'd love to.* C *Planning a party* D *Birthdays*	**Students can …** ☑ talk about their plans for specific dates ☑ accept or decline an invitation ☑ discuss and agree on plans ☑ describe birthday traditions in their culture	*Be going to* *Yes / no* questions *Wh-* questions with *be going to* Object pronouns	Months and dates Party checklist

Functional language	Listening and Pronunciation	Reading and Writing	Speaking
Interactions: Expressing dislikes Expressing likes	**Listening:** Food preferences A typical Swedish meal **Pronunciation:** Word Stress	**Reading:** "My Favorite Food" An article **Writing:** A typical meal	• Survey about meals • *Keep talking*: Recipes • Information exchange about food preferences • Comparison of eating habits • *Keep talking*: Discussion about eating habits • Interview about favorite food
Interactions: Asking for directions	**Listening:** GPS directions Tourist information **Pronunciation:** Word stress	**Reading:** "Escape Rooms" A magazine article **Writing:** Group poster	• Information exchange with maps • *Keep talking*: Information gap activity with neighborhood maps • Role play about directions • Interview about places in town • *Keep talking*: Description of an unusual zoo • Presentation about a city attraction
Interactions: Asking if someone can talk now Explaining that you can't talk now	**Listening:** Sound effects Telephone calls **Pronunciation:** Intonation in questions	**Reading:** "Status Updates" A micro-blog **Writing:** My status update	• Guessing game about people's actions • *Keep talking*: Interpretations of actions • Role play of a phone call • "Find someone who" activity about things people are doing these days • *Keep talking*: Guessing game about who's doing what • Speculations about someone's activities
Interactions: Showing that you're listening Expressing surprise	**Listening:** Diana's week Matt's busy week **Pronunciation:** Simple past *-ed* endings	**Reading:** "Matt's Movie Reviews" Blog post **Writing:** A blog post	• Information exchange about last weekend • *Keep talking*: Picture story • Role play of surprising conversations • Interview about routine events in the past • *Keep talking*: Memories • "Find someone who" activity about past activities
Interactions: Reacting to good news Reacting to bad news	**Listening:** A short trip Three vacations **Pronunciation:** Reduction of *did you*	**Reading:** "Travel Tales" Blog posts **Writing:** A postcard	• Interview about where you were • *Keep talking*: Interview about school trips • Class exchange of personal news • Information exchange about vacations • *Keep talking*: Speculation about a vacation • Presentation of postcards
Interactions: Declining an invitation Accepting an invitation	**Listening:** Invitations A "Sweet 16" birthday party **Pronunciation:** Reduction of *going to*	**Reading:** "Birthday Traditions" An article **Writing:** A thank-you note	• Information exchange about special days • *Keep talking*: Weekend plans • Class invitations • Discussion of plans for three scenarios • *Keep talking*: Plan for a party • Discussion about birthday traditions

Welcome

1 Introducing yourself

A 🎧 Listen and practice.

> **Simon** Hello. I'm Simon.
> **Chen** Hi, Simon. My name is Chen.
> Nice to meet you.
> **Simon** Nice to meet you, too.

B `PAIR WORK` Introduce yourselves.

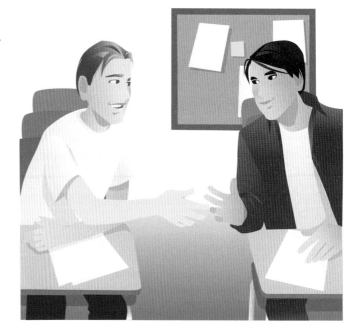

2 Introducing someone else

A 🎧 Listen and practice.

> **Simon** Chen, this is my friend Sofia.
> **Sofia** Hi, Chen. Nice to meet you.
> **Chen** Nice to meet you, too, Sofia.

B `GROUP WORK` Introduce your partner from Exercise 1 to another classmate.

3 Hi and bye

A 🎧 Listen and practice.

Simon Hi, Chen!
Chen Good morning, Simon! How are you?
Simon I'm fine, thanks. And you?
Chen Fine, thank you.

Simon See you later, Chen!
Chen Bye, Simon!

B 🎧 Listen to the expressions. Then practice the conversation again with the new expressions.

Saying hello
Hi.
Hello.
Good morning.
Good afternoon.
Good evening.

Saying good-bye
Bye.
Good-bye.
See you.
See you later.
See you tomorrow.

C **CLASS ACTIVITY** Say hello to your classmates and ask how they are. Then say good-bye.

I can introduce myself and others. ✓
I can say hello and good-bye. ✓

3

Classroom language 🎧

Pair work

Group work

Class activity

Compare answers.

Cover the picture.

Go to page 12.

Ask and answer questions.

Interview your partner.

Role-play the situation.

7 Food

Warm Up

A Match the words and the pictures.

1 Italian food ___C___   2 Mexican food _____   3 Chinese food _____   4 Japanese food _____

B Name ten food words you know.

A Breakfast, lunch, and dinner

1 Vocabulary Food

A 🎧 Match the words and the pictures. Then listen and check your answers.

a	apples	e	carrots	i	eggs	m	pasta
b	bananas	f	cereal	j	fish	n	potatoes
c	beans	✓g	cheese	k	milk	o	rice
d	beef	h	chicken	l	noodles	p	tomatoes

Dairy

1 g
2

Vegetables

3
4
5

Fruit

6
7

Grains

8
9
10
11

Meat and Protein

12
13
14
15
16

B **PAIR WORK** Do you ever eat the food in Part A? Tell your partner.

"I often eat apples. I sometimes eat eggs. I never eat noodles."

2 Language in context Favorite meals

A 🎧 Listen to three people talk about their favorite meals. Underline the food.

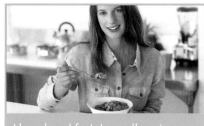

I love breakfast. I usually eat some cereal, but I don't have any milk with it. I also eat an apple.

My favorite meal is lunch. I don't have a lot of time, so I often just get some noodles.

My favorite meal of the day is dinner. A typical dinner for me is rice and beans with some beef.

B What about you? What's your favorite meal of the day? What do you eat?

3 Grammar 🎧 Count and noncount nouns; *some* and *any*

Count nouns	Noncount nouns
an apple apples a tomato tomatoes	milk rice

Do you have **any** apples?
   Yes, I have **some** (apples).
   No, I don't have **any** (apples).

Do you have **any** milk?
   Yes, I have **some** (milk).
   No, I don't have **any** (milk).

A Complete the chart with the food words from Exercise 1. Then compare with a partner.

Count nouns		Noncount nouns	
apples	_____	milk	_____
tomatoes	_____	cereal	_____
_____	_____	_____	_____
_____	_____	_____	_____

B Circle the correct words. Then practice with a partner.

A What do you want for lunch, Amy?

B Let's just make **some** / **any** pasta.

A Good idea. We have **some** / **any** pasta.

B Let's see. We have **some** / **any** carrots.
    We don't have **some** / **any** tomatoes.

A OK, I can get **some** / **any** at the store. What else?

B Do we have **some** / **any** cheese?

A No, we don't have **some** / **any**. I can get **some** / **any**.

C PAIR WORK Practice the conversation again.
Use other food words from Exercise 1.

4 Speaking What do you eat?

A Write your answers to the questions in the chart.

What do you often eat for ... ?	Me	Name: _____	Name: _____
breakfast			
lunch			
dinner			

B GROUP WORK Interview two classmates. Complete the chart with their answers.

5 Keep talking!

Go to page 139 for more practice.

I can say what meals I eat. ✓

3 I like Chinese food!

1 Interactions Likes and dislikes

A Look at the pictures. Where are Maria and Tom?

B 🎧 Listen and practice.

Maria	Look! They have Italian food here.
Tom	Do you like Italian food?
Maria	I don't like pizza at all, but I love pasta.
Tom	I don't like Italian food.

Maria	How about Chinese food?
Tom	Good idea. I like Chinese food!
Maria	I really like the noodles here.
Tom	Great! We can eat lunch at this restaurant.

C 🎧 Listen to the expressions. Then practice the conversation again with the new expressions.

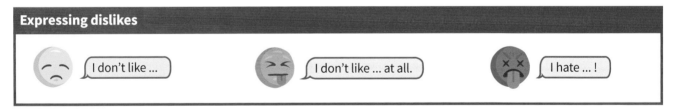

Expressing dislikes

I don't like …   I don't like … at all.   I hate … !

Expressing likes

I like …   I really like …   I love … !

D **PAIR WORK** Look at Maria's and Tom's likes and dislikes. Are they the same as yours? Tell your partner.

	😍	😄	🙂	🙁	😖	😣
Maria	fish	Mexican food	Japanese food	milk	beans	beef
Tom	cheese	carrots	Chinese food	Italian food	French food	eggs

"Maria loves fish, but I don't like fish at all."

2 Pronunciation Word stress

A 🎧 Listen and repeat. Notice the stress in the words.

●	●•	•●•
cheese	**a**pple	ba**na**na
beans	**chi**cken	po**ta**to
beef	**noo**dles	to**ma**to
_____	_____	_____
_____	_____	_____

B 🎧 Listen. Complete the chart with the correct words.

> dairy   fruit   Italian   meat   pasta

3 Listening I love it!

A 🎧 Listen to four conversations about food. Check (✓) the words you hear.

1 ☐ beans   2 ☐ cheese   3 ☐ noodles   4 ☐ bananas
   ☑ beef   ☐ chicken   ☐ potatoes   ☐ carrots
   ☑ pasta   ☐ eggs   ☐ tomatoes   ☐ cereal

B 🎧 Listen again. Do the two speakers like the same things? Circle the correct answers.

1 yes / (no)   2 yes / no   3 yes / no   4 yes / no

4 Speaking What do you like?

A Make a list of food you like and food you don't like.

Food I like
🙂
😄
😍

Food I don't like
🙁
😖
😵

B **PAIR WORK** Tell your partner about the food you like and don't like. Ask and answer questions for more information.

A: I really like fish.
B: Do you cook fish at home?
A: No, I don't. I eat fish in restaurants.

I can say what I like and dislike. ✓

69

C Meals

1 Vocabulary More food

A 🎧 Label the pictures with the correct words. Then listen and check your answers.

| dumplings | ✓ hot dogs | pizza | soup | sushi |
| hamburgers | pancakes | salad | spaghetti | tacos |

1 _hot dogs_   2 _____   3 _____   4 _____   5 _____

6 _____   7 _____   8 _____   9 _____   10 _____

B **PAIR WORK** Which food in Part A do you like? Which food don't you like? Compare your answers.

A: I really like dumplings. Do you?

B: Yes, I like dumplings, too. Do you like … ?

2 Conversation I eat pizza every day.

🎧 Listen and practice.

Megan What is that?

David Pizza. My father is a pizza chef.

Megan Really? So how often do you eat pizza?

David I eat pizza every day. It's my favorite food!

Megan I don't eat pizza very often, but it looks interesting. What's on it?

David Cheese, tomatoes, black beans, and fish.

Megan Yuck!

David Have some. It's really good.

Megan No, thanks. I'm not very hungry.

3 Grammar 🎧 *How often; time expressions*

How often do you eat pizza?	
I eat pizza	every day. once a week. twice a month. three times a month. once in a while.	I don't eat pizza **very often**. I **never** eat pizza.

A Look at Matt's menu. Answer the questions. Then practice with a partner.

WEEKLY MENU PLANNER
Matt's menu

	Monday	Tuesday	Wednesday	Thursday	Friday	Saturday	Sunday
Breakfast	cereal	eggs	cereal	eggs	cereal	pancakes	pancakes
Lunch	soup	pizza	soup	sushi	soup	tacos	sushi
Dinner	dumplings	chicken	beef	chicken	pizza	spaghetti	hamburgers

1 How often does Matt eat hamburgers for dinner? *He eats hamburgers once a week.*
2 How often does Matt eat soup for lunch?
3 How often does Matt eat pancakes?
4 How often does Matt eat hot dogs?
5 How often does Matt eat sushi for lunch?
6 How often does Matt eat dumplings for dinner?

B PAIR WORK Make six sentences about your eating habits with different time expressions. Tell your partner.

"I eat spaghetti once a month."

4 Speaking Eating habits

A Add three food words to the chart. Then answer the questions.

B PAIR WORK Interview your partner. Complete the chart with his or her answers.

C PAIR WORK Compare your information with another partner.

"Kazu eats hot dogs once a week, but I eat them once in a while."

How often do you eat ...?	Me	Name:
hot dogs		
salad		
tacos		

5 Keep talking!

Go to page 140 for more practice.

I can talk about my eating habits.

71

D Favorite food

1 Reading 🎧

A Look at the pictures in the magazine article. Can you name the food?

B Read the article. What's the best title? Check (✓) the correct answer.

☐ Meal Times ☐ My Favorite Food ☐ Dinner Around the World

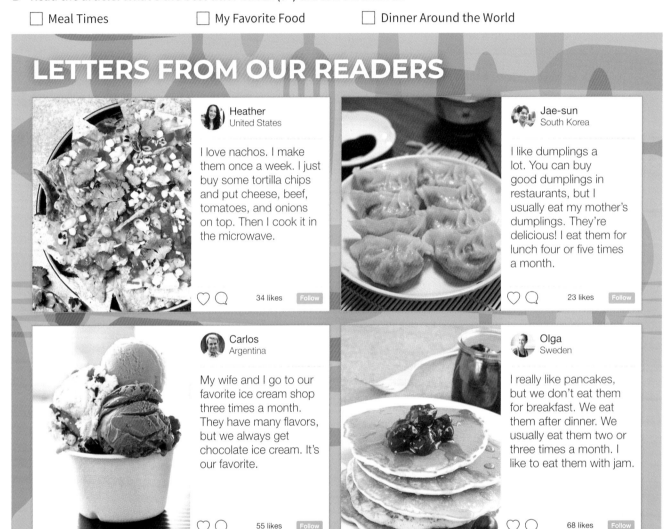

LETTERS FROM OUR READERS

Heather
United States

I love nachos. I make them once a week. I just buy some tortilla chips and put cheese, beef, tomatoes, and onions on top. Then I cook it in the microwave.

♡ ◯ 34 likes Follow

Jae-sun
South Korea

I like dumplings a lot. You can buy good dumplings in restaurants, but I usually eat my mother's dumplings. They're delicious! I eat them for lunch four or five times a month.

♡ ◯ 23 likes Follow

Carlos
Argentina

My wife and I go to our favorite ice cream shop three times a month. They have many flavors, but we always get chocolate ice cream. It's our favorite.

♡ ◯ 55 likes Follow

Olga
Sweden

I really like pancakes, but we don't eat them for breakfast. We eat them after dinner. We usually eat them two or three times a month. I like to eat them with jam.

♡ ◯ 68 likes Follow

C Read the article again. Complete the chart with the correct information.

Name	Favorite food	How often they have it
Heather	nachos	once a week
Jae-sun		
Carlos		
Olga		

D **PAIR WORK** Imagine you can have one food in Part A right now. Which food do you want? Why? Tell your partner.

"I want dumplings. I love South Korean food. Vegetable dumplings are my favorite."

2 **Listening** A meal in Sweden

A 🎧 Listen to Olga describe a typical meal in Sweden. Which meal does she talk about? Check (✓) the correct answer.

☐ breakfast ☐ lunch ☐ dinner

B 🎧 Listen again. Circle the words you hear.

beans	(bread)	cheese	fish	milk	pancakes
beef	cereal	eggs	fruit	noodles	potatoes

3 **Writing** A typical meal

A Think of a typical meal in your country. Answer the questions.

1 What do people drink? _____
2 What do people eat? _____
3 Do *you* usually eat it? _____
4 Why or why not? _____

B Write about a typical meal in your country. Use the model and your answers in Part A to help you.

C **CLASS ACTIVITY** Post your writing around the room. Read your classmates' writing. Who describes similar meals?

A Japanese Breakfast

People in Japan usually drink green tea for breakfast. They eat fish, rice, soup, salad, and pickles. It's a healthy and delicious breakfast, but I don't eat this. I usually drink orange juice and eat cereal and fruit for breakfast.

4 **Speaking** What's your favorite meal?

A **PAIR WORK** Add two questions about food to the chart. Then interview your partner. Take notes.

Questions	Name: _____
What's your favorite meal?	
What's your favorite kind of food?	
How often do you have it?	
Who makes it?	
Can you cook it?	
What do you drink with it?	

A: What's your favorite kind of food?

B: I love Mexican food.

B **GROUP WORK** Tell your group about your partner's favorite meal. Do you like that meal, too? Does your group like it?

I can talk about my favorite food. ✓

Wrap-up

1 Quick pair review

Lesson A `Brainstorm!`

Make a list of count and noncount food words. How many do you know? You have two minutes.

Lesson B `Do you remember?`

Look at the pictures. Complete the sentences with the correct words. You have one minute.

I _don't like_ fish _at all_ .

I _____ French food.

I _____ beef.

I _____ breakfast.

I _____ milk!

I _____ carrots!

Lesson C `Find out!`

What is one thing both you and your partner eat every week? Eat once in a while?
Never eat? You have two minutes.

A: I eat rice every week. Do you?

B: Yes, I do.

Lesson D `Guess!`

Describe your favorite food, but don't say its name! Can your partner guess what it is?
Take turns. You have two minutes.

A: I love this food. It's Italian, and I eat it once in a while. I eat it at home.

B: Is it pasta?

A: Yes.

2 In the real world

Go online and find information in English about your favorite movie star's or musician's
eating habits. Then write about them.

- What is his or her favorite food?
- How often does he or she usually eat it?

Bruno Mars's Favorite Food

The American musician Bruno Mars loves
chicken adobo. It's chicken with rice, and it's
the national dish of the Philippines.

8 In the neighborhood

LESSON A	LESSON B	LESSON C	LESSON D
• Places in the neighborhood • Prepositions of location	• Asking for directions	• Places to visit • *There is, there are*	• Reading: "Escape Rooms" • Writing: Group poster

Warm Up

A Look at the pictures. Where can you do these things?

buy flowers	buy some vegetables	find an ATM	eat lunch	see a doctor	see a movie

B What other places can you find in a city?

"You can find a police station."

A Around town

1 Vocabulary Places in the neighborhood

A 🎧 Match the words and the places. Then listen and check (✓) your answers.

a	bank	c	bus stop	e	gas station	g	library	i	subway station
b	bookstore	✓d	coffee shop	f	hotel	h	newsstand	j	supermarket

B PAIR WORK Which places are in your school's neighborhood?

"We have a coffee shop, some restaurants, and a …"

2 Language in context Ads

A 🎧 Read three advertisements for places in a neighborhood. What places do they describe?

Mama's Place

Come to Mama's Place for real Italian food.

On Second Avenue | 10% off between 5:30 and 6:30 p.m.

Find everything you need at **ABC Supermarket.**
New location next to Town Bank

We're always open!

Joe's Coffee Shop

Find us on the corner of **Main Street and First Ave.**
Best coffee in town!

B What can you do at each place in Part A?

3 Grammar 🎧 Prepositions of location

in   on   next to

across from   between   on the corner of

The newsstand is **in** the park.

The gas station is **on** Second Avenue.

The supermarket is **next to** the bank.

The bus stop is **across from** the park.

The hotel is **between** the restaurant and the bookstore.

The coffee shop is **on the corner of** Main Street and First Avenue.

Look at the map in Exercise 1. Complete the sentences with the correct prepositions.

1   The newsstand is _____*in*_____ the park.

2   The subway station is _____ the park.

3   The bookstore is _____ the hotel.

4   Mama's Place is _____ Second Avenue.

5   The gas station is _____ Second Avenue and Grand Street.

6   The library is _____ the coffee shop and the bus stop.

4 Pronunciation Word stress

🎧 **Listen and repeat. Notice the stress on the first or last syllable.**

● •		• ●
bookstore	**news**stand	a**cross**
coffee	**sta**tion	be**tween**
corner	**sub**way	ho**tel**

5 Speaking Where's the drugstore?

A **PAIR WORK** **Add these four places to the map in Exercise 1. Then ask and answer questions about their locations.**

drugstore

post office

police station

department store

A: Where's the drugstore on your map?

B: It's next to the bank. Where is it on your map?

B **PAIR WORK** **Where are the places in your town? Tell your partner.**

6 Keep talking!

Student A go to page 141 and Student B go to page 142 for more practice.

I can give the locations of neighborhood places. ✓

How do I get to ...?

1 Giving directions

A 🎧 Listen and repeat.

1

Go up Main Street.

Turn left on Ninth Street.

Go one block.

It's **on the right**, next to a school.

2

Walk down Main Street.

Take a right on Fifth Street.

Walk two blocks.

It's **on the left**, across from the park.

B **PAIR WORK** Give directions from *Start* to the coffee shop and the bus station.

2 Interactions Directions

A 🎧 Listen and practice.

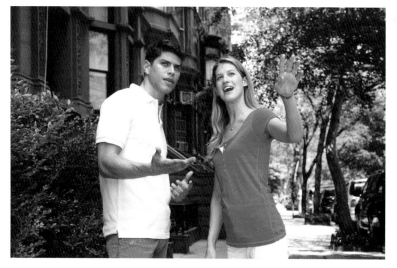

Alex	Excuse me. How do I get to the park?
Laura	Go down Seventh Street and take a left on Elm Street. Walk one block to Sixth Street. It's on the right, across from the bus station.
Alex	Turn left on Elm Street?
Laura	Yes.
Alex	Great! Thank you very much.

B 🎧 Listen to the expressions. Then practice the conversation again with the new expression.

Asking for directions

How do I get to ... ?

How can I get to ... ?

3 Listening Follow the route

A 🎧 Listen to Carl and Alice use their GPS to get from Pioneer Square to the library in Seattle. Follow their route. Then mark an X at the library.

B 🎧 Listen to Carl and Alice go from the library to Pike Place Market. Follow their route. Then mark a ✓ at the market.

C PAIR WORK Give directions from Pioneer Square to other places on the map. Your partner follows them. Take turns.

4 Speaking How do I get to ...?

A PAIR WORK Draw a simple map of the neighborhood around your school. Label different places and street names.

B PAIR WORK Role-play the situation. Then change roles.

Student A: You are a tourist in town. Ask for directions to places in the neighborhood.

Student B: You meet a tourist in your town. Give him or her directions to places in your neighborhood. Start at your school.

A: How do I get to the train station?

B: Walk down Main Street . . .

I can ask for and give directions. ✓

C Fun in the city

1 Vocabulary Places to visit

A 🎧 Listen and repeat.

amusement park

aquarium

movie theater

museum

science center

swimming pool

water park

zoo

B PAIR WORK How often do you go to each place? Tell your partner.

"Our town has a swimming pool, but I hardly ever go there."

2 Conversation Tourist information

🎧 Listen and practice.

Larry   Hello. Can I help you?

Maggie   Yes. Is there a museum near here?

Larry   Let's see ... yes. There's a museum across from the park.

Maggie   And is there an aquarium in this city?

Larry   Yes, there is. It's near the museum. It's a very nice aquarium.

Maggie   Great. I have one more question. Are there any amusement parks?

Larry   There aren't any amusement parks, but there's a nice water park.

3 Grammar 🎧 *There is, there are*

There's a museum.	**There are** two swimming pools.
There isn't an amusement park.	**There aren't** any good zoos in this city.
Is there an aquarium in this city?	**Are there** any swimming pools near here?
Yes, **there is.** No, **there isn't.**	Yes, **there are.** No, **there aren't.**
Contraction There's = There is	

A Complete the questions about the city with *Is there a / an … ?* or *Are there any … ?*
Then compare with a partner.

1 Is there a _____ zoo?

2 _____ water parks?

3 _____ aquarium?

4 _____ museums?

5 _____ amusement park?

6 _____ movie theaters?

B **PAIR WORK** Ask and answer the questions in Part A.
Use the map on the right.

A: Is there a zoo?

B: Yes, there is. There's one zoo.

4 Speaking Is there . . . ? Are there . . . ?

A **PAIR WORK** Add two items to the chart. Then interview your partner. Check (✓) the places
that are in his or her neighborhood, and ask for more information.

	Places	Locations	Extra information
☐	movie theaters		
☐	museums		
☐	science center		
☐	swimming pool		
☐			
☐			

A: Are there any movie theaters in your neighborhood?

B: Yes, there's one. It's on University Avenue.

A: How often do you go there?

B **CLASS ACTIVITY** Tell the class about two interesting places in your partner's neighborhood.

5 Keep talking!

Go to page 143 for more practice.

I can talk about interesting places in my town. ✓

D A great place to visit

1 Reading 🎧

A What are your favorite places to visit?

B Read the article. Where is the world's first escape room?

ESCAPE ROOMS

Imagine! You are in a room with nine other people. Is it a hotel room, an old library, or even a castle? The door is closed, and you can't leave ...

Your job: find a key and escape the room. You have only 60 minutes. Is this a movie, a video game, or a bad dream? No – it's an escape room!

Every day, thousands of people visit escape rooms in cities around the world. To find the key and win the game, players answer questions and do puzzles. Players

share information and work in pairs or in groups – you need a team to escape the room!

In some games, there is only one room. In others, you travel through many rooms to escape. Sometimes there are even actors in the room to help you! Some rooms are simple, and most players escape in less than 60 minutes. But some are very difficult, and players hardly ever escape in time.

The world's first escape room is in Japan. But, today, there are more than 2,800 games in many countries.

C Read the article again. Answer the questions.

1 What do players find to escape a room?   Players find a key.
2 How many people visit escape rooms every day?
3 How long do players have to escape?
4 How do players find the key to the door?
5 Who sometimes help the players?
6 How many escape rooms are there in the world?

D **PAIR WORK** Do you want to visit an escape room? Why or why not?
What's another fun adventure that you like?

2 Listening City information

A 🎧 Listen to three tourists ask for information about two places in the city. Write the places in the chart.

	Place 1	Place 2
1	(movie theater)	
2		
3		

B 🎧 Listen again. Which places are in the city? Circle the correct answers.

3 Writing and speaking Group poster presentation

A GROUP WORK Choose an interesting place in your city. What do you know about it? Make a list.

B GROUP WORK Create and design a poster about the place. Use your list from Part A.

COME TO THE IMAGINE SCIENCE CENTER!

GREAT FOR KIDS, TEENS, AND ADULTS.

WE'RE OPEN EVERY DAY FROM 9:00 TO 6:00. • THERE'S A FREE AUDIO TOUR IN TEN LANGUAGES. THERE'S AN EXCELLENT CAFÉ IN THE MUSEUM. • TRY OUR SCIENCE EXPERIMENTS. LEARN ABOUT PLANT LIFE. • THERE ARE OVER 10,000 BOOKS IN THE BOOKSTORE.

C CLASS ACTIVITY Present your posters. Ask and answer questions for more information.

A: The Imagine Science Center is a great place to visit.

B: It's open every day from 9:00 to 6:00.

C: There's a free audio tour. You can listen to the tour in ten languages.

D: Where is the Imagine Science Center?

C: It's at 367 First Avenue, near the park.

Wrap-up

1 Quick pair review

Lesson A `Brainstorm!`

Make a list of places in a neighborhood. How many do you know? You have one minute.

Lesson B `Do you remember?`

Circle the correct answers. You have two minutes.

A Excuse me. **Where** / (**How**) do I get to the library from here?

B Walk up Third Avenue and **turn** / **take** left on Elm Street.

A Is the library on Elm Street?

B No, It's not. **Go** / **Turn** two blocks on Elm Street. Then **take** / **walk** a right on Main Street. The library is **on** / **in** the right.

A Thanks!

Lesson C `Find out!`

What are two kinds of places both you and your partner like to visit in your city? What are two kinds of places you don't like to visit? You have two minutes.

A: I like museums. Do you?

B: Not really. How about water parks? I love those!

A: I do, too!

Lesson D `Guess!`

Describe a place to visit in your area, but don't say its name! Can your partner guess the name? Take turns. You have two minutes.

A: I go there with my friends on weekends.

B: Is it Mall Marina?

A: No. There are rides and games there.

B: Is it the amusement park, Fantasy Land?

A: Yes!

2 In the real world

What zoos do you know? Go online and find information in English about a zoo. Then write about it.

- What is the name of the zoo? Where is it?
- What animals and exhibits are there?
- Can you watch videos or take a tour on the website?

The San Diego Zoo

The San Diego Zoo is a famous zoo in California. You can see pandas there. You can also …

9 What are you doing?

Warm Up

A Look at the pictures. Make six sentences about them.

B Which of these things do you do every day?

A I'm looking for you.

1 Vocabulary Actions and prepositions

A 🎧 Listen and repeat.

start

hold

look for

wave

sit

stand

run

end

B 🎧 Listen and repeat.

behind

in

in front of

on

under

C **PAIR WORK** Tell your partner to sit and stand in different places in the classroom.
Use the prepositions. Take turns.

"Stand in front of the door."

2 Language in context Meeting a friend

A 🎧 Listen to Amy and Claudio meet at a soccer game. Where is Amy? Where is Claudio?

Amy	Hi, Claudio. It's Amy. I'm standing under the scoreboard. Where are you?
Claudio	I'm sitting in front of the big clock. Do you see me?
Amy	No, I don't.
Claudio	Well, I'm wearing a red shirt.
Amy	But, Claudio, everyone is wearing a red shirt!

B What about you? Where do you usually meet your friends
at big games or other events?

3 Grammar 🎧 Present continuous statements

I'm **standing** under the scoreboard.	I'm **not sitting**.	*Spelling*
You're **running**.	You're **not walking**.	run → run**ning**
He's **sitting** in front of the big clock.	He's **not standing**.	sit → sit**ting**
It's **starting**.	It's **not ending**.	wave → wav**ing**
We're **holding** scarves.	We're **not waving**.	
They're **playing** soccer.	They're **not playing** tennis.	

A Complete Claudio's text messages with the present continuous forms of the verbs.

Where are you, Tim?
I'*m looking*_____ (look) for you.
The game _____
(start), but my favorite player
_____ (not / play) right
now. Please text me.

Amy and I _____ (watch)
the game. But where are you,
Tim? We _____ (sit) in
row 56. Wait! I _____
(get) a message. Is it you?

Amy and I _____ (hold)
signs. We _____ (wave)
in front of the TV cameras.
Can you see us?

B **PAIR WORK** Make ten sentences about people in your class with the present continuous. Tell your partner.

"I'm sitting behind Eva. Lily and Mei are wearing sweaters."

4 Listening Someone is ...

🎧 Listen to the sound effects. What is happening? Circle the correct answers.

1 Someone is (watching a game) / watching a movie.
2 Someone is **getting up** / **going to bed**.
3 Someone is **walking** / **running**.

4 Some people are **playing tennis** / **playing soccer**.
5 The game is **starting** / **ending**.

5 Speaking Guess the action.

GROUP WORK Perform an action. Your group guesses it. Take turns.

cook	run	stand
play tennis	sit	watch TV
play the guitar	sleep	wave

A: You're dancing.
B: No, I'm not.

A: You're playing soccer.
B: Yes, that's right.

6 Keep talking!

Go to page 144 for more practice.

I can describe what people are doing right now. ✓   87

B I can't talk right now.

Interactions Can you talk?

A Look at the pictures. What is Amanda doing?

B 🎧 Listen and practice.

Amanda	Hello?
Justin	Hi, Amanda. It's Justin. Is this a good time to talk?

Amanda	Oh, sorry. I can't talk right now. I'm cooking dinner. Can I call you back?
Justin	OK, sure. Talk to you later.
Amanda	Thanks. Bye.

C 🎧 Listen to the expressions. Then practice the conversation again with the new expressions.

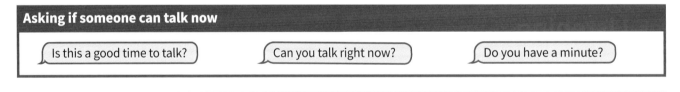

Asking if someone can talk now

Is this a good time to talk?	Can you talk right now?	Do you have a minute?

Explaining that you can't talk now

I can't talk right now.	I'm busy right now.	This isn't a good time.

D **PAIR WORK** Practice the conversation again with the reasons below.

clean	do my homework	watch a movie	wait for the doctor

2 **Listening** Do you have a minute?

A 🎧 **Listen to four phone conversations. Number the questions you hear from 1 to 4.**

_____ Can you talk right now?   _____ Is this a good time to talk?

_____ Is this a good time?   ___1___ Do you have a minute?

B 🎧 **Listen again. Why can't each person talk right now? Write the reason.**

1 Eric ___is having dinner___ .   3 Ji-won _____ .

2 Renee _____ .   4 Carmen _____ .

3 **Speaking** Role play

A **Complete the sentences with reasons why you can't talk on the phone.**

I'm watching _____ .   I'm eating _____ .

I'm studying _____ .   I'm _____ .

B **PAIR WORK** **Role-play the situations. Then change roles.**

Student A: Answer the phone. Explain that you can't talk now and say why. Use the reasons from part A.

Student B: Call Student A. Identify yourself and ask if he or she can talk right now.

I can ask if someone can talk now. ✓

I can explain why I can't talk on the telephone. ✓

C These days

1 Vocabulary Activities

A 🎧 Listen and repeat.

create a website

learn to drive

look for a job

study for an exam

study Italian

take a dance class

take tennis lessons

tutor a student

B **PAIR WORK** Which activities are fun? Which are not fun? Compare answers with a partner.

2 Conversation Old friends

🎧 Listen and practice.

Jill Long time no see, Wendy!

Wendy Oh, hi, Jill!

Jill What are you doing these days?

Wendy I'm learning to drive. I'm also tutoring a student. Oh, and I'm taking a dance class.

Jill You sound really busy.

Wendy I am. How about you, Jill? Are *you* doing anything special these days?

Jill Yes, I am. I'm studying Italian.

Wendy Really? Why are you studying Italian?

Jill Because ... Oh, my phone is ringing. Hello? Sorry, Wendy. It's my new friend, Luigi.

Wendy Oh.

Jill *Ciao, Luigi! Come stai?*

3 Grammar 🎧 Present continuous questions

What **are** you **doing** these days? I**'m learning** to drive. What class **is** Wendy **taking**? She**'s taking** a dance class. Where **are** they **studying**? They**'re studying** online.	**Are** you **doing** anything special these days? Yes, I **am**. No, I**'m not**. **Is** she **tutoring** a student? Yes, she **is**. No, she**'s not**. **Are** they **taking** tennis lessons? Yes, they **are**. No, they**'re not**.

A Complete the questions with the present continuous forms of the verbs. Then compare with a partner.

1 _____Are_____ you _____taking_____ (take) music lessons these days?

2 What classes _____ you _____ (take)?

3 _____ you and your friends _____ (buy) new music these days?

4 What _____ your classmates _____ (learn) in this class?

5 What languages _____ you _____ (study)?

6 _____ you _____ (learn) to drive?

B PAIR WORK Ask and answer the questions in Part A. Answer with your own information.

4 Pronunciation Intonation in questions

🎧 Listen and repeat. Notice the intonation of *yes / no* and *Wh-* questions.

Are you watching a lot of TV? ↗

What TV shows are you watching? ↘

5 Speaking Busy lives

CLASS ACTIVITY Add two activities to the chart. Then find classmates who are doing each thing these days. Write their names and ask questions for more information.

Are you ... these days?	Name	Extra information
studying another language		
reading a good book		
watching a lot of TV		
taking any fun classes		
streaming a lot of music		

6 Keep talking!

Go to page 145 for more practice.

I can describe what people are doing these days. ✓

D What's new?

1 Reading

A What are you and your classmates doing right now?

B Read the status updates. Which two people are waiting for other people?

WHAT'S YOUR STATUS?

🔍   SIGN UP   LOGIN

Type your message
here and hit enter

 Donna Bristol   I'm standing under the JB Cola sign on Main Street. I'm waiting for my friend Hank. But Hank is never late! Hank?
APR 19 8:33 P.M.

 Hank Jones   I'm standing in line. Donna, please wait!! I'm in a store on First Avenue. The line isn't moving.
APR 19 8:50 P.M.

 Fernando Sanchez   I'm studying English. I'm doing grammar exercises online. I'm getting them all correct. Yay!
APR 19 9:05 P.M.

 Zack Parker   I'm enjoying Singapore!! I love vacations! How are my friends in Chicago doing?
APR 19 9:17 P.M.

 Hee-jin Park   I'm having a great evening. I'm at my favorite restaurant with my two friends, Alex and Eddie. We're waiting for dessert.
APR 19 9:28 P.M.

 Jessica King   I'm looking for a good French dictionary. I'm taking a French class and need help with my vocabulary.
APR 19 9:44 P.M.

 Arthur Henderson   I'm waiting for my daughter to come home. It's almost 10:00 p.m. Where are you, Lisa? You know the rules!
APR 19 9:58 P.M.

 Lisa Henderson   I'm at a basketball game. Sorry, Dad. My favorite player is playing. 15 more minutes?
APR 19 10:02 P.M.

C Read the updates again. Complete the sentences with first names.

1 ___Zack___ is on vacation.

2 _____ is having dinner.

3 _____ is standing in line.

4 _____ is watching a basketball game.

5 _____ and _____ are students.

6 _____ and _____ are late.

D **PAIR WORK** How often do you write messages like the ones above? What do you write about? Tell your partner.

"I love status updates. I write them twice a day. I usually write about the new music I find online."

2 **Writing** My status update

A Write or tell your classmates in a group chat what you're doing right now or these days.

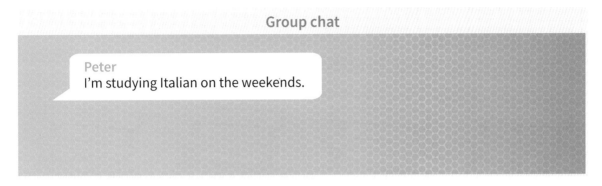

Group chat

> **Peter**
> I'm studying Italian on the weekends.

B **GROUP WORK** Pass your paper to the classmate on your right or send an update to the group. Read and respond to your classmate's update. Continue to pass, read, and respond to each classmate's update three times with different actions.

Group chat

> **Peter**
> I'm studying Italian on the weekends.

> **Michelle**
> I'm not studying Italian, but I'm learning to drive.

3 **Speaking** Makoto's Desk

GROUP WORK Look at Makoto's desk. What do you think he's doing these days?

A: I think he's studying French.

B: Right. And he's playing tennis.

C: Do you think he's drinking a lot of coffee?

I can discuss what people are doing. ✓

Wrap-up

1 Quick pair review

Lesson A Do you remember?

Complete the sentences with the correct prepositions. You have one minute.

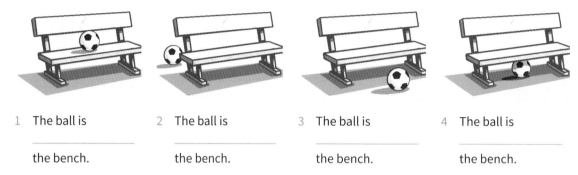

1 The ball is
_____
the bench.

2 The ball is
_____
the bench.

3 The ball is
_____
the bench.

4 The ball is
_____
the bench.

Lesson B Brainstorm!

Make a list of phone expressions. How many do you know? You have two minutes.

Lesson C Find out!

What are two things both you and your partner are doing these days? You have one minute.

A: What are you doing these days?

B: I'm taking tango lessons. Are you?

A: No, I'm not.

Lesson D Guess!

Describe the clothes and actions of someone in your class, but don't say his or her name!
Can your partner guess the name? Take turns. You have two minutes.

A: He's wearing a baseball cap and talking to Angela right now.

B: Is it Sebastian?

A: Yes, it is.

2 In the real world

Go to a mall or park. What are people doing? Write about them.

People in the Park

I am in the park. Two women are walking. One woman is wearing a red T-shirt. A man is sitting next to me. He is eating his lunch. He is also …

10 Past experiences

A — Benjamin, age 16

B — Benjamin, age 43

C — Luz, age 14

D — Luz, age 29

Warm Up

A Look at the pictures. Make three sentences about each one.

B How are *you* different now?

A Last weekend

1 Vocabulary Weekend activities

A 🎧 **Listen and repeat.**

listen to music

play basketball

play in a band

shop for new clothes

stay home

stay out late

visit relatives

watch an old movie

B **PAIR WORK** **Do you do any of the activities in Part A? When do you do them? Tell your partner.**

"My friends and I usually play basketball on Saturday mornings."

2 Language in context Carmen's weekend

A 🎧 **Listen to Carmen talk about last weekend. Number the pictures from 1 to 3.**

1 Last Saturday morning, my brother Pedro called me. We talked for hours. I uploaded some photos, and I listened to music.

2 I stayed out late on Saturday night. Pedro and I watched an old movie. We laughed a lot. We loved it!

3 On Sunday afternoon, I stayed home. I watched another movie. I didn't like the ending at all. I cried.

1

B **What about you? What do you usually do on weekends?**

3 Grammar 🎧 Simple past regular verbs

		Spelling
I **listened** to music last Saturday.	I **didn't watch** a movie.	stay → stay**ed**
You **stayed** home.	You **didn't stay** out late.	love → lov**ed**
He **called** me on Saturday.	He **didn't call** me on Sunday.	cry → cr**ied**
We **laughed**.	We **didn't cry**.	shop → shop**ped**
They **stayed** out late.	They **didn't stay** at home.	

A Write sentences about the things Pedro did and didn't do last weekend.

Things to Do

✓ call Carmen   ✗ listen to music

✓ watch a movie   ✓ upload photos

✗ play basketball   ✗ shop for new clothes

1 *Pedro called Carmen.*

2 _____

3 _____

4 _____

5 _____

6 _____

B **PAIR WORK** Make true sentences about your weekend with the past forms of the verbs in Part A. Tell your partner.

4 Pronunciation Simple past -*ed* endings

A 🎧 Listen and repeat. Notice that some verbs have an extra syllable in the past tense.

Same syllable (most verbs)		Extra syllable (verbs ending in *t* and *d*)	
call / called		chat / chat·ted	
listen / listened		start / start·ed	
play / played		upload / upload·ed	

B 🎧 Listen. Complete the chart with the correct verbs.

download / downloaded	shop / shopped	visit / visited
post / posted	stay / stayed	watch / watched

5 Speaking A fun weekend

A Complete the phrases with your own ideas.

chat with _____   exercise _____   study _____   visit _____

cook _____   look for _____   talk to _____   walk to _____

B **PAIR WORK** Tell your partner about the things you did and didn't do last weekend. Use the phrases from Part A to help you.

A: I chatted online with my friends last weekend. How about you?

B: I didn't chat online with my friends, but I called them.

6 Keep talking!

Go to page 146 for more practice.

I can say what I did last weekend. ✓

B You're kidding!

1 Interactions Expressing surprise

A Look at the pictures. What do you think Diego and Jasmine are talking about?

B 🎧 Listen and practice.

Diego I checked plane tickets to go to Walt Disney World in May.

Jasmine Uh-huh.

Diego They're usually $600, but right now they're $350!

Jasmine You're kidding!

Diego I know. I didn't buy them, but I called my parents, and they liked the idea.

Jasmine That's great. I love that place.

C 🎧 Listen to the expressions. Then practice the conversation again with the new expressions.

Showing that you're listening
Uh-huh.   Oh?   Oh, yeah?

Expressing surprise
Really?   What?   You're kidding!

D **PAIR WORK** Check (✓) the best responses. Then practice with a partner.

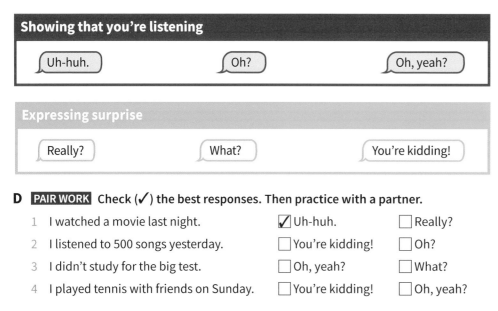

1 I watched a movie last night.   ✓ Uh-huh.   ☐ Really?
2 I listened to 500 songs yesterday.   ☐ You're kidding!   ☐ Oh?
3 I didn't study for the big test.   ☐ Oh, yeah?   ☐ What?
4 I played tennis with friends on Sunday.   ☐ You're kidding!   ☐ Oh, yeah?

2 Listening What a week!

A 🎧 Listen to Diana tell her friend about the past week. Number the pictures from 1 to 4.

B 🎧 Listen again. What surprises Diana's friend? Complete the sentences.

1 Diana didn't _____*answer*_____ three _____*questions*_____.

2 Diana's _____ boyfriend _____ her.

3 Julie didn't _____ the _____.

4 Diana _____ home on _____.

3 Speaking Really?

A Match the sentences. Then compare with a partner.

1 Last night, I studied for my English test for five hours. ___*b*___   a I watched them with my dad.

2 I just checked my email. _____   b But I didn't get a good score.

3 Last week, I streamed two movies. _____   c I'm learning Chinese.

4 On Thursday, I started a new class. _____   d I have 100 new messages.

B **PAIR WORK** Role-play the situations in Part A. Then change roles.

Student A: Say the lines from Part A.

Student B: Show interest or express surprise.

A: Last night, I studied for my English test for five hours, but I didn't get a good score.

B: You're kidding! Why not?

C **PAIR WORK** Role-play new situations. Use your own ideas.

I can show that I'm listening. ✓

I can express surprise. ✓

99

C Did you make dinner last night?

1 Vocabulary Things to do

A 🎧 Listen and repeat.

do laundry

do the dishes

get a haircut

go grocery shopping

have a party

make dinner

see a play

see friends

sleep

B **PAIR WORK** How often do you do the things in Part A? Tell your partner.

"I *do laundry once a week. I do the dishes every day* ..."

2 Conversation Last night

🎧 Listen and practice.

Mindy	Hi, Pete. Did you see Jennifer last night?
Pete	Yes, I did. But the day didn't go so well.
Mindy	Really? What happened?
Pete	Well, I did my laundry yesterday morning, but my favorite white shirt turned pink.
Mindy	You're kidding!
Pete	Then I got a haircut, but I really didn't like it.
Mindy	Oh, yeah? Did you make dinner for Jennifer?
Pete	Well, I slept for a while, so I didn't go grocery shopping.
Mindy	Oh. Did you eat anything?
Pete	Yeah, we did. Jennifer bought a pizza for us.
Mindy	Really?

3 Grammar 🎧 Simple past irregular verbs; *yes* / *no* questions

I **saw** Jennifer last night.	I **didn't see** Jennifer last week.	**Did** you **see** Jennifer last night?
She **bought** a pizza.	She **didn't buy** soup.	Yes, I **did.** No, I **didn't.**
They **ate** a pizza.	They **didn't eat** salad.	**Did** she **buy** dinner?
		Yes, she **did.** No, she **didn't.**
		Did they **eat** dinner?
		Yes, they **did.** No, they **didn't.**

A Complete the conversation with the simple past tense form of the verbs. Then practice with a partner.

A Hey, Pablo. _____Did_____ you _____do_____ (do) today's homework?

B I _____. I _____ (not / have) time.

A Really? Why not?

B I _____ (see) some friends yesterday. We _____ (eat) lunch, and then we _____ (go) to the mall.

A Oh, yeah? _____ you _____ (buy) any clothes?

B I _____ (not / buy) anything! So, _____ you _____ (do) *your* homework?

A Yes, I did. And no, you can't see it!

> 🎧 **Common irregular verbs**
>
> | | |
> |---|---|
> | buy → **bought** | have → **had** |
> | do → **did** | make → **made** |
> | drink → **drank** | meet → **met** |
> | drive → **drove** | read → **read** |
> | eat → **ate** | see → **saw** |
> | fall → **fell** | sleep → **slept** |
> | get → **got** | take → **took** |
> | go → **went** | write → **wrote** |
>
> *Go to page 152 for a list of more irregular verbs.*

B Put the words in order to make questions. Then compare with a partner.

1 last night / you / see / did / your friends   *Did you see your friends last night?* _____

2 go / last weekend / you / did / grocery shopping _____

3 watch / you / a movie / did / last night _____

4 yesterday / stay home / you / did _____

5 make dinner / did / on Thursday / you _____

6 you / did / last Saturday / have a party _____

C **PAIR WORK** Ask and answer the questions in Part B. Answer with your own information.

A: *Did you see your friends last night?*

B: *Yes, I did. I saw two friends. We ate out at a restaurant.*

4 Speaking Did you?

A **PAIR WORK** Add two past time expressions to the list. Then ask and answer *Did you ... ?* questions with each time expression. Take notes.

A: *Did you make dinner last night?*

B: *Yes, I did. Did you do laundry last night?*

A: *No, I didn't.*

Past time expressions	
last night	last week
yesterday	last weekend

B **GROUP WORK** Tell your group about your partner's answers. Did anyone do anything interesting?

5 Keep talking!

> Go to page 147 for more practice.

D I saw a great movie.

1 Reading

A Do you read the review of a movie before you watch it? Or do you think it spoils the fun?

B Read Matt's review and the comments people made. Who liked the movie?

HOME   REVIEWS   CONTACT ME

Matt's Movie Reviews

Too Young to Love
On Friday, my friend Naomi and I hung out together. We had a very good time. We saw a great old movie at the Cineplex. They are showing old movies all month. Did anyone see *Too Young to Love?* I loved it! It's a story about two young people who are in love. Their parents think they are too young, so they can't get married. It's not a sad movie. It's really funny! We laughed a lot.
MONDAY, 11:00

CGIRL   I saw *Too Young to Love.* I also saw the play. Both are good. See the movie and the play.
MONDAY, 11:26 A.M

OSCAR   *Too Young to Love*?! You're kidding! I hated the movie, but I liked the music. The sound track had some really good old songs. MONDAY, 1:00 P.M.

TOMAS   My friend and I saw it. She laughed. I cried because I paid for the tickets, and I didn't like it at all. TUESDAY, 7:00 A.M.

JOE C   I liked *Too Young to Love.* I saw three old movies at the Cineplex last month, and I really liked all of them. TUESDAY, 12:45 P.M.

MARIA   What?! *Too Young to Love*?! I hated the movie, but I loved the book. TUESDAY, 1:15 P.M.

C Read the blog again. Correct the false sentences.

1 Matt saw the movie on ~~Saturday~~.   Matt saw the movie on Friday.

2 Oscar hated the music.

3 Tomas liked *Too Young to Love*.

4 Joe C didn't see any movies at the Cineplex last month.

5 Maria hated the book *Too Young to Love*.

D **PAIR WORK** Do you or your friends ever post reviews of movies, food, or places you visit online? What do you post about? Tell your partner.

"My friend Rosa reviews every restaurant she goes to. She is a hard critic!"

2 **Writing** A blog post

A Choose one day last week. Complete the chart with information about the things you did that day.

Day	Activities	Places	Other information

B Write a blog post about that day. Use the model and your answers in Part A to help.

C PAIR WORK Share your post. Ask and answer questions for more information.

"Did you have a good time? Did you eat out?"

Friday

After class, I met my friend Terry. We went shopping at the mall. I bought a new watch. I didn't pay much for it, but I really like it. I went home at 8:00 p.m.

3 **Listening** A busy week

A 🎧 Listen to Matt talk about last week. What activities did he do? Check (✓) the correct answers.

☐ did laundry ☐ made dinner ☐ read books
✓ got up early ☐ played soccer ☐ stayed out late
☐ got up late ☐ played the guitar ☐ worked

B 🎧 Listen again. What activities did Matt enjoy? Circle the activities above.

4 **Speaking** I played in a band last year.

A CLASS ACTIVITY Add two past activities to the chart. Then find classmates who did each thing. Write their names and ask questions for more information.

Find someone who …	Name	Extra information
bought a cell phone last year		
got a haircut last week		
saw a friend yesterday		
made dinner last night		
watched a game on TV last weekend		
wrote a blog post yesterday		

A: Did you buy a cell phone last year, Alex?
B: Yes, I did.

B GROUP WORK Share your information.

"Alex bought a cell phone last year."

I can talk about past activities. ✓ 103

Wrap-up

1 Quick pair review

Lesson A `Find out!`

What are three things both you and your partner did after class yesterday?
What are three things you didn't do? You have two minutes.

A: I walked home after class yesterday. Did you?

B: Yes, I did. I watched TV at home. Did you?

A: No, I didn't. I listened to music.

Lesson B `Do you remember?`

Circle the correct answers. You have two minutes.

1 A I listened to all of Taylor Swift's songs today.

   B Oh? / You're kidding! All of them?
      She has a lot!

2 A Janet uploaded photos from the party.

   B Uh-huh. / Really? I know. I looked at them
      this morning.

3 A Charlie's band played at The Red Room
      downtown on Saturday night!

   B What? / Oh? No way! That's so cool!
      I didn't know that.

4 A I visited my grandmother last weekend.

   B You're kidding! / Oh, yeah? How is she doing?

Lesson C `Test your partner!`

Say eight irregular verbs in the simple present. Can your partner write the simple past forms
of the verbs correctly? Check his or her answers. You have two minutes.

1 _____   3 _____   5 _____   7 _____

2 _____   4 _____   6 _____   8 _____

Lesson D `Guess!`

Make two true sentences and one false sentence about your activities last week. Can your
partner guess the false sentence? Take turns. You have two minutes.

A: I watched 20 movies last week. I played basketball in the park. I saw a play.

B: You didn't watch 20 movies.

A: You're right. I only watched 12.

2 In the real world

Did anyone else do the same things as you yesterday? Go online and find three English-speaking
bloggers who did the same activities as you yesterday. Then write about them.

- What activities did both you and the bloggers do yesterday?
- What are the bloggers' names? Where are they from?

Bloggers and Me

I played basketball yesterday. Three bloggers also played basketball yesterday.
Diego is from California. He played basketball with his brother.

11 Getting away

Warm Up

A Do you know any of these places? Which ones?

B What are some popular places to visit in your country? In your city?

A Where were you?

1 Vocabulary Adjectives

A 🎧 Listen and repeat.

exciting / fun / great

all right / OK / so-so

awful / terrible

boring

interesting

noisy

quiet

B PAIR WORK Think of things that each adjective describes. Discuss your ideas.

A: *Sports are exciting.*

B: *Basketball is exciting, but I think soccer is boring.*

2 Language in context Quick getaways

A 🎧 Listen to four people talk about recent trips. Number the pictures from 1 to 4.

1 We went on a school trip last week. We went to a theater and saw an exciting play. The actors were great.

–Olivia

2 We just had a three-day weekend. I went away with my family. It was a fun trip, but our hotel wasn't very nice. In fact, it was terrible.

–Ichiro

3 I was at my brother's apartment last weekend. He doesn't have a TV or a computer. It was quiet and kind of boring.

–Brian

4 My friend and I went on a day trip last week. We took a local bus to an old town. The bus was awful and noisy, but the trip was interesting. Look what I bought!

–Eleanor

1

B Did each person like his or her trip? Why or why not?

3 Grammar 🎧 Past of *be*

Where were you last weekend?	**Was** your trip interesting?
I **was** at my brother's apartment.	Yes, it **was**.　No, it **wasn't**.
How was your weekend?	**Were** the people nice?
It **was** quiet and kind of boring.	Yes, they **were**.　No, they **weren't**.

I / he / she / it	*you / we / they*	*Contractions*	
was	**were**	wasn't = was not	weren't = were not

A Complete the guest comment card with *was*, *were*, *wasn't*, or *weren't*. Then compare with a partner.

Guest comments

My wife, son, and I ____were____ guests at your hotel last week. Unfortunately, we _____ happy with our room. The room _____ clean, and the beds _____ awful. And the room _____ near the street. The noise _____ terrible in the early morning. But the people at the hotel _____ great, so that _____ good!

B Read the answers. Write the questions. Then practice with a partner.

1. How was your weekend? — It was great.
2. _____ — Yes, my weekend was interesting.
3. _____ — I was on a trip.
4. _____ — No, I wasn't at the theater on Friday.
5. _____ — Yes, I was at home on Sunday afternoon.
6. _____ — My parents were in Tahiti.

C PAIR WORK Ask and answer the questions in Part B. Answer with your own information.

4 Speaking Where were you last Friday night?

A PAIR WORK Interview your partner. Take notes.

Where were you ... ?	Location	Extra information
at this time yesterday		
on your birthday		
on New Year's Eve		
last Friday night		

B GROUP WORK Tell your group about your partner's answers. Who was in an interesting place? Who did interesting things?

5 Keep talking!

Go to page 148 for more practice.

I can describe where I was in the past.

107

B That's great!

1 Good news, bad news

A 🎧 Listen and repeat.

I got a promotion.   I lost my wallet.   I missed my flight.   I was sick.   I won a contest.

B **PAIR WORK** Which things are good news? Which are bad news? Can you think of other examples? Discuss your ideas.

2 Interactions Reacting to news

A 🎧 Listen and practice.

Meg	Did you have a good weekend?	Joe	And how was your weekend?
Joe	Yes! It was my sister's birthday, so we went to the beach.	Meg	It wasn't so good. I lost my phone.
Meg	Really? That's great!	Joe	Oh, no! What happened?

B 🎧 Listen to the expressions. Then practice the conversation again with the new expressions.

Reacting to good news

That's great!   That's excellent!   That's awesome!

Reacting to bad news

Oh, no!   That's too bad.   That's terrible!

C **PAIR WORK** Practice the conversation again with the examples from Exercise 1. React to the news.

A: Did you have a good weekend?

B: Yes! I got a promotion, so I went shopping.

3 **Listening** A short trip

A 🎧 Listen to Sam tell a friend about a short trip. Number the pictures from 1 to 6.

B 🎧 Listen again. Was Sam's trip great, good, bad, or awful?

4 **Speaking** That's ... !

A Write three good things and three bad things that happened to you last week.

	Good things that happened	Bad things that happened
1		
2		
3		

B CLASS ACTIVITY Ask your classmates about their week. React to the news.

A: Did you do anything interesting last week?

B: Well, I started a new job.

A: That's excellent!

B: Yeah. But I lost my cell phone.

A: That's terrible!

C My vacation

1 Vocabulary Vacation activities

A 🎧 Listen and repeat.

buy souvenirs

go sightseeing

go to a festival

go to the beach

relax

shop in markets

take a tour

take pictures

B **PAIR WORK** Did you do any of the activities in Part A on your last vacation? Tell your partner.

"On my last vacation, I bought souvenirs and took pictures. I didn't go to the beach."

2 Conversation Back from vacation

🎧 Listen and practice.

Dave How was your vacation, Kate?

Kate Oh, it was exciting. We had a great time.

Dave Where did you go?

Kate I went to Veracruz, Mexico.

Dave That's great. Who did you travel with?

Kate My sister.

Dave When did you get back?

Kate Last night. I got home at midnight.

Dave Really? That's late! So, what did you do there?

Kate Well, we went to a festival called *Carnaval*. We also shopped in local markets and took lots of pictures. Look, I bought you a souvenir.

Dave Thanks! I love it!

3 Grammar 🎧 Simple past *Wh-* questions

Where did you **go** on vacation?
  I went to Veracruz, Mexico.
When did you **get** back?
  Last night.
Who did you **travel** with?
  My sister.
	What did you **do** there?
	  We went to a festival and shopped.
	Why did you **go** to Veracruz?
	  Because the festival is famous.
	How did you **get** to Veracruz?
	  By plane.

Match the questions and the answers. Then practice with a partner.

1 Where did you go on vacation? __f__
2 Who did you go with? _____
3 When did you get back? _____
4 What did you do on vacation? _____
5 Why did you go to Vietnam? _____
6 How did you travel in Vietnam? _____

a We got back last week.
b We took the bus and the train.
c We relaxed and took pictures.
d Because I have friends there.
e I went with my brother.
f I went to Vietnam.

4 Pronunciation Reduction of *did you*

A 🎧 **Listen and repeat. Notice how** *did you* **is pronounced /dɪdʒə/ after**
Wh- **question words.**

  Where **did you** go?   What **did you** do?   When **did you** get back?

B PAIR WORK Practice the questions in the grammar chart. Reduce *did you*
to /dɪdʒə/ after *Wh-* question words.

5 Speaking What a vacation!

A Answer the questions.

- Where did you go on your last vacation? _____
- Who did you go with? _____
- When did you go? _____
- What did you do there? _____
- How did you travel? _____
- Did you buy anything? _____
- What did you like about the vacation? _____
- What didn't you like about the vacation? _____

B GROUP WORK Tell your group about your last vacation.
Ask and answer questions for more information.

6 Keep talking!

Go to page 149 for more practice.

fly → flew

take a boat → took a boat

I can talk about my last vacation. ✓

D Travel experiences

1 Reading 🎧

A How often do you go on vacation? Where do you go?

B Read the travel blog posts. What country is each person visiting?

TRAVEL TALES

I'm here in Chiang Mai, Thailand. Yesterday, I went on a short elephant ride. There was a man on the elephant in front of me. His name was Alan Johnson. My name is Alan Johnson, too!
POSTED ON OCTOBER 12, 10:30 A.M.
ALAN JOHNSON

My sister and I are in Paris, France. It's our first trip overseas. We went to an outdoor café the other day, and Johnny Depp was at the next table. How exciting!
POSTED ON OCTOBER 14, 6:48 P.M.
MARY O'CONNOR

I'm here with my parents at a hotel in Miami, Florida. We came to visit our relatives. We all went to bed last night at about midnight. At 3:00 in the morning, we heard a fire alarm.
POSTED ON OCTOBER 15, 8:06 A.M.
ANITA GONZALEZ

I'm in Granada, Nicaragua. I came here to help build houses. It's a great country. We finished our first house yesterday. We're not staying in a hotel. We're staying in a school.
POSTED ON OCTOBER 21, 9:12 P.M.
DIANE NICHOLSON

C Read the blog posts again. What is the last sentence of each post? Number the posts from 1 to 4.

1 Last night, we all slept in one big room!

2 He was nice to us, and I have a cool photo now.

3 I can't believe that we have the same name!

4 We ran down to the street and were fine.

D **PAIR WORK** What adjectives describe each travel experience? Discuss your ideas.

A: I think Alan Johnson's trip was very exciting!

B: Me, too. I love elephants, and Thailand is an interesting country.

2 Listening Three different trips

A 🎧 Listen to three people talk about their vacations. How do they describe them? Check (✓) the correct answers.

	How were their vacations?		What was one thing they liked?
1	☐ awful	✓ great	shopping
	☐ boring	☐ so-so	
2	☐ fun	☐ OK	
	☐ interesting	☐ terrible	
3	☐ awful	☐ exciting	
	☐ boring	☐ great	

B 🎧 Listen again. What did they like about their trips? Write one thing for each person in the chart.

3 Writing and speaking A postcard

A Read Sofia's postcard to Jack about her vacation.

Dear Jack,

Linda and I are having a great time here in Morocco. We took a train from Casablanca to Marrakech yesterday. Last night, we went to a big "souk," or market. We walked around the market for hours! I bought a nice souvenir for you.

See you soon!
Sofia

B Write a postcard to a friend or family member about an experience you had on vacation. Use the model in Part A to help you.

C CLASS ACTIVITY Post your postcards around the room. Read your classmates' postcards. Then write questions about five postcards that interest you.

1. Eddie – What did you buy for your sister?
2. Jung-woo – Who did you travel with?
3. Marcus – When did you take this vacation?

D CLASS ACTIVITY Find the classmates who wrote the five postcards. Ask them your questions.

A: Eddie, what did you buy your sister?

B: I bought a scarf.

A: I see, thanks. Excuse me, Jung-woo, who did you travel with?

I can describe a vacation. ✓

Wrap-up

1 Quick pair review

Lesson A `Brainstorm!`

Make a list of adjectives. How many do you know? You have one minute.

Lesson B `Do you remember?`

Check (✓) the correct answers. You have one minute.

1 I won a free ticket to Jamaica.   ☑ That's great!   ☐ Oh, no!

2 I lost my cell phone.   ☐ That's terrible!   ☐ That's excellent!

3 My sister missed her flight.   ☐ That's awesome.   ☐ That's too bad.

4 Charlie met Leonardo DiCaprio.   ☐ Oh, no!   ☐ That's great!

Lesson C `Find out!`

What are two things both you and your partner did on your last vacation?
You have two minutes.

A: Did you go sightseeing on your last vacation?

B: Yes, I did. How about you?

A: Yes, I went sightseeing, too.

Lesson D `Test your partner!`

Describe a vacation. Can your partner draw a postcard of your vacation?
Check his or her drawing. You have two minutes.

"Last year, my sister and I went to Madrid, Spain.
We shopped in El Rastro Market and went to
art museums."

2 In the real world

Do you ever read travel blogs? Go online and find
a travel blog in English. Then write about it.

- Where did the blogger go?
- When did he or she go there?
- What did he or she do there?

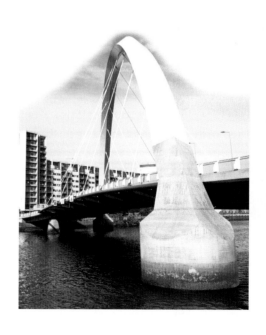

Kelly's Travel Blog

Kelly is a blogger from Canada. Last week, she
went on vacation to Scotland. She went
sightseeing in Glasgow. She went to ...

12 Time to celebrate

wedding

Warm Up

A Label the pictures with the correct words.

> birthday   graduation   holiday   ✓ wedding

B What special events do you celebrate?

A I'm going to get married.

1 Vocabulary Months and dates

A 🎧 Listen and repeat.

January	February	March	April	May	June
July	August	September	October	November	December

1st	first	**9th**	ninth	**17th**	seventeenth	**25th**	twenty-fifth
2nd	second	**10th**	tenth	**18th**	eighteenth	**26th**	twenty-sixth
3rd	third	**11th**	eleventh	**19th**	nineteenth	**27th**	twenty-seventh
4th	fourth	**12th**	twelfth	**20th**	twentieth	**28th**	twenty-eighth
5th	fifth	**13th**	thirteenth	**21st**	twenty-first	**29th**	twenty-ninth
6th	sixth	**14th**	fourteenth	**22nd**	twenty-second	**30th**	thirtieth
7th	seventh	**15th**	fifteenth	**23rd**	twenty-third	**31st**	thirty-first
8th	eighth	**16th**	sixteenth	**24th**	twenty-fourth		

B **CLASS ACTIVITY** When is your birthday? Stand in the order of your birthdays, from the first to the last in the year.

A: My birthday is July twenty-eighth.

B: Mine is July twentieth. You're next to me.

2 Language in context Special days

A 🎧 Listen to three people talk about special days. What are the dates of the special days?

I'm going to graduate from high school on June 8th. I'm going to start college in September.

–Sarah

My eightieth birthday is on August 21st. I'm going to go skydiving for the first time. I can't wait!

–Walter

My boyfriend, Kenta, and I are going to get married on October 16th. We're going to have a big wedding.

–Mari

B What about you? What days of the year are special to you? Why?

116

3 Grammar 🎧 *Be going to*; *yes* / *no* questions

I'm **going to graduate** on June 8th.	**Are** you **going to start** college?
I'm **not going to start** college in July.	Yes, I am. No, I'm not.
Walter**'s going to go** skydiving.	**Is** Walter **going to go** skydiving?
He**'s not going to play** basketball.	Yes, he is. No, he isn't.
Mari and Kenta **are going to get** married.	**Are** they **going to have** a big wedding?
They**'re not going to have** a small wedding.	Yes, they are. No, they aren't.

A Complete the conversation with the correct forms of *be going to*.
Then practice with a partner.

A _____*Are*_____ you __*going to graduate*__ (graduate)
from college this year?

B Yeah, on May 30th. My parents _____ (have)
a big party for me.

A Great! _____ the party _____ (be)
at their house?

B No, it _____ (not / be) at the house.
They _____ (have) it at a restaurant.

A _____ you _____ (get) a job right away?

B No, I'm not. First, I _____ (travel).
Then I _____ (look) for a job.

B **PAIR WORK** Ask and answer three *Are you going to … ?* questions.
Answer with your own information.

4 Pronunciation Reduction of *going to* before verbs

A 🎧 Listen and repeat. Notice how *going to* is reduced to /gənə/ in informal
spoken English.

Are you **going to** do anything special?   Yes. I'm **going to** go skydiving.

B **PAIR WORK** Practice the sentences in the grammar chart. Reduce *going to*
to /gənə/.

5 Speaking Three special days

A Write the dates and your plans for three special days or holidays next year.

	Special day: _____ .	Special day: _____	Special day: _____
Dates			
Plans			

B **PAIR WORK** Tell your partner about your special days. Ask and answer questions for more information.

6 Keep talking!

Go to page 150 for more practice.

I can talk about my plans for specific dates. ✓

B Sure. I'd love to.

1 Interactions Invitations

A How often do you go to the movies with your friends?

B 🎧 Listen and practice.

Bill	Hello?
Brandon	Hey, Bill. It's Brandon. Listen, do you want to see a movie tonight?
Bill	Tonight? I'm sorry. I can't.
Brandon	Oh, OK. Well, maybe some other time.

Melissa	Hello?
Brandon	Hi, Melissa. This is Brandon. Do you want to see a movie tonight?
Melissa	A movie? Sure. I'd love to.
Brandon	Great.

C 🎧 Listen to the expressions. Then practice the conversation again with the new expressions.

Declining an invitation

I'm sorry. I can't.	I'm afraid I can't.	I'm really sorry, but I can't.

Accepting an invitation

Sure. I'd love to.	Sounds good.	Yeah. That sounds great.

D **PAIR WORK** Practice the conversations again with the activities below.

get some ice cream	hang out	play video games	watch TV

A: Hello?

B: Hey, Bill. It's Brandon. Listen, do you want to get some ice cream tonight?

2 Listening I'd love to, but …

A 🎧 Listen to four people invite their friends to do things tonight. Number the pictures from 1 to 4.

B 🎧 Listen again. Do the friends accept or decline the invitations? Check (✓) the correct answers.

1	✓ accept	2	☐ accept	3	☐ accept	4	☐ accept
	☐ decline		☐ decline		☐ decline		☐ decline

3 Speaking Do you want to hang out?

CLASS ACTIVITY "Call" your classmates and invite them to do something with you right now. Your classmates accept the invitations or decline them with excuses. Use the ideas below or your own ideas.

Possible things to do	Possible excuses	Responses to excuses
go out for coffee	I'm cooking dinner.	Oh, that's OK.
go to a party	I'm not feeling well.	Maybe next time.
see a movie	I'm eating lunch.	I'm sorry you can't make it.
go to the mall	I'm studying for an exam.	OK, I understand.
hang out	I'm doing my homework.	That's all right.
go shopping	I'm working late tonight.	No problem.

A: Hello?

B: Hi, it's me. Do you want to go to the mall?

A: I'm really sorry, but I can't. I'm not feeling well.

B: OK, I understand. Maybe next time.

I can accept or decline an invitation. ✓

C Planning a party

1 Vocabulary Party checklist

A 🎧 Match the things on the checklist and the pictures. Then listen and check your answers.

THINGS TO DO

1 ☑ bake a cake
2 ☐ buy a gift
3 ☐ choose the music
4 ☐ decorate the room
5 ☐ make a guest list
6 ☐ plan the menu
7 ☐ prepare the food
8 ☐ send invitations

a

b

c

d

e

f

g

h

B PAIR WORK When is a good time to do each thing in Part A? Discuss your ideas.

2 weeks before the party	2–3 days before the party	the morning of the party
1 week before the party	the day before the party	1 hour before the party

"A good time to make a guest list is two weeks before the party."

2 Conversation I can bake!

🎧 Listen and practice.

Andrea We have a lot of things to do for Eric's birthday party. Look, I made a checklist.

Mark Good idea. Who's going to help us?

Andrea Rosario. She's going to send the invitations.

Mark How is she going to send them?

Andrea By email.

Mark Good. That's easy. What are we going to buy for Eric?

Andrea Let's get him a sweater.

Mark Great. Who's going to bake the cake?

Andrea I'm going to bake it.

Mark Um, do you think that's a good idea?

Andrea Hey, I can bake!

Mark OK.

3 Grammar 🎧 *Wh-* questions with *be going to*; object pronouns

What are we going to buy **Eric**?		Let's get **him** a sweater.
Who's going to bake **the cake**?		Andrea's going to bake **it**.
How is she going to send **the invitations**?		She's going to send **them** by email.

	I	you	he	she	it	we	they
Subject	I	you	he	she	it	we	they
Object	me	you	him	her	it	us	them

A Complete the conversation with the correct forms of *be going to*. Then practice with a partner.

A What time _____*are*_____ you ___*going to go*___ (go) to Eric's birthday party?

B _____ (go) to the party at 6:45.

A How _____ you _____ (get) there?

B My friend Jason _____ (drive). Do you want a ride?

A Um, sure, thanks! What _____ you _____ (do) after the party?

B Jason and I _____ (go) out. I think we _____ (see) a movie.

B Rewrite the sentences. Use object pronouns. Then compare with a partner.

1 He's not going to invite Mary.   *He's not going to invite her.*

2 Let's call Bill and Ami again.   _____

3 I'm going to see Eric tomorrow.   _____

4 He's going to help Debbie and me.   _____

5 We're going to buy the present tomorrow.   _____

6 Call Rosario at 5:00.   _____

C **CLASS ACTIVITY** Ask your classmates what they're going to do tonight. Answer with your own information.

4 Speaking Let's decide together.

A **PAIR WORK** Discuss the situations.

Your classmate Masao is in the hospital. He has nothing to do. What are you going to bring him?

You're planning your friend's birthday party. Where is it going to be? What are you going to eat and drink?

You want music for your teacher's birthday party. What songs are you going to play? How are you going to listen to them?

A: What are we going to bring to Masao?

B: Let's bring him a new video game.

A: That's a great idea. How about … ?

B **GROUP WORK** Share your ideas with another pair. Ask and answer questions for more information.

5 Keep talking!

Go to page 151 for more practice.

I can discuss and agree on plans. ✓

121

D Birthdays

1 Reading 🎧

A What was the last party you went to? What did you do at the party?

B Read the article. Which birthdays are special in each country?

NIGERIA
In Nigeria, the first, fifth, tenth, and fifteenth birthdays are very special. To celebrate these birthdays, people have big parties and invite up to 100 people. They eat "jollof rice." This is rice with tomatoes, red peppers, onions, and cassava, a kind of potato.

JAPAN
The third, fifth, and seventh birthdays are very important in Japan. Every year on November 15th, three-year-old boys and girls, five-year-old boys, and seven-year-old girls celebrate the *Shichi-go-san* (Seven-five-three) Festival. They usually wear traditional clothes and eat "thousand-year candy" for a long life.

BIRTHDAY TRADITIONS AROUND THE WORLD

ECUADOR
In Ecuador, a family has a big party when a girl turns 15 years old. The birthday girl wears a dress, and her father puts her first pair of high-heeled shoes on her. Then he dances with her. Fourteen other girls dance with fourteen other boys at the same time.

SOUTH KOREA
Parents in South Korea sometimes try to guess a child's future on his or her first birthday. They put the child in front of some objects, such as a book and a coin. They wait to see which object the child takes. For example, a book means the child is going to be a teacher. A coin means the child is going to have a lot of money.

C Read the article again. Answer the questions.

1 On special birthdays, what do Nigerian children eat? _They eat "jollof rice."_

2 Who celebrates *Shichi-go-san*? _____

3 Who dances with a 15-year-old Ecuadorian girl at her birthday party? _____

4 How do South Korean parents guess a child's future? _____

D `PAIR WORK` How did you celebrate your last birthday? Tell your partner.

"I celebrated my last birthday with my friends. We ate out at a nice restaurant."

2 Listening Sweet 16

A 🎧 **Listen to Amanda, a 16-year-old American girl, describe her "Sweet 16" birthday party. Check (✓) the true sentences.**

1 ✓ Amanda's birthday is July 14th.

2 ☐ ~~Her parents~~ made a guest list. *She*

3 ☐ She sent the invitations.

4 ☐ She and her father decorated the room.

5 ☐ She had pizza, ice cream, and cake.

6 ☐ Forty of her friends came.

7 ☐ She got a gift from her parents.

8 ☐ She's going to have a party on her 18th birthday.

B 🎧 **Listen again. Correct the false sentences.**

3 Writing A thank-you note

A **Think of a birthday gift (or any gift) you received. Answer the questions.**

- What is the gift? _____
- Who is it from? _____
- Why did you get it? _____
- What do you like about it? _____

B **Write a thank-you note for the gift. Use the model and your answers in Part A to help you.**

C GROUP WORK **Share your thank-you notes. Did any of you write about similar gifts?**

> Dear Liz,
>
>   Thanks a lot for the birthday gift. I love the sweater. Blue and green are my favorite colors. Thank you for coming to my party!
>
>   Thanks again,
>   Sun-hee

4 Speaking How we celebrate

A GROUP WORK **Discuss the ways people celebrate birthdays in your culture. Use the questions below and your own ideas.**

- Which birthdays are very special?
- Do people celebrate with family, friends, or both?
- What do people eat and drink?
- What do people do?
- Do they give gifts? What kinds of gifts?
- How do you usually celebrate birthdays?

B GROUP WORK **Tell your group how you are going to celebrate your next birthday. Are you going to do any of the things you discussed in Part A?**

a birthday party in Mexico

I can describe birthday traditions in my culture. ✓

Wrap-up

1 Quick pair review

Lesson A `Guess!`

Say three dates when you are going to do something special. Can your partner guess what you are going to do? Take turns. You have three minutes.

A: I'm going to do something special on June 17th.

B: Are you going to graduate?

A: Yes, I am!

Lesson B `Do you remember?`

Read the sentences. Write A (accepting an invitation), D (declining an invitation), or E (making an excuse). You have one minute.

1   I'd love to. _____
2   I'm studying for an exam. _____
3   That sounds great. _____

4   I'm really sorry, but I can't. _____
5   I'm working late tonight. _____
6   I'm afraid I can't. _____

Lesson C `Brainstorm!`

Make a list of things you do to plan a party. How many do you know?
You have two minutes.

Lesson D `Find out!`

What are three activities both you and your partner do on your birthdays?
You have two minutes.

A: I eat cake on my birthday. Do you?

B: Yes, I eat cake, too.

2 In the real world

When is your birthday? Go online and find information in English about two important events that happened that day. Then write about them.

- Where did the events happen?
- Who participated in the events?
- Why were the events important?

My Birthday

My birthday is December 17th. On this day in 1903, the Wright brothers flew an airplane for 12 seconds. This was important because ...

What's in your shopping basket?

A Choose seven items to put into your shopping basket. Circle them.

B PAIR WORK Find out what is in your partner's basket. Can you make the dishes below with the food in your baskets?

Stew
beef
carrots
noodles

Fruit
smoothie
apples
bananas
milk

Spaghetti
and
meatballs
beef
cheese
pasta
tomatoes

A: I have beef and noodles. Do you have any carrots?

B: Yes, I do. We can make stew!

C PAIR WORK What else can you make with the food in your baskets?

How often do you eat standing up?

GROUP WORK Add two eating habits to the list. Then discuss how often you do each thing.

drink coffee in the morning

drink tea

eat alone

eat junk food in class

eat fast food for breakfast

eat on the street

eat standing up

_____
(your own idea)

_____
(your own idea)

A: Do you ever drink coffee in the morning?

B: Yes, I do.

C: How often do you drink coffee in the morning?

B: I drink coffee in the morning three times a week. How about you?

Keep talking!

What's missing?

Student A

A **PAIR WORK** You and your partner have pictures of the same neighborhood, but different places are missing. Ask questions to get the names. Write them.

A: What's next to the supermarket?

B: The gas station.

B **PAIR WORK** Cover the picture. Tell your partner six things you remember.

A: The gas station is next to the supermarket.

B: That's right.

What's missing?

Student B

A PAIR WORK You and your partner have pictures of the same neighborhood, but different places are missing. Ask questions to get the names. Write them.

A: *What's across from the post office?*

B: *Parkview Hotel.*

B PAIR WORK Cover the picture. Tell your partner six things you remember.

A: *Parkview Hotel is across from the post office.*

B: *That's right.*

Keep talking!

An unusual zoo

PAIR WORK What's wrong at this zoo? Make ten sentences about the people, animals, and other things in the zoo. Use *There is ...* , *There are ...* , and prepositions of location.

"There's a bear in the car."

Neighbors

A **PAIR WORK** Look through the windows. What are the people doing? Discuss your ideas.

A: I think the man is doing his homework. What do you think?

B: I think he's writing a letter. He's sitting, too.

B **PAIR WORK** What are the people actually doing? Go to page 153 to check your answers.

Keep talking!

Who is it?

A Write three sentences about what you're doing these days on three pieces of paper. Don't write your name!

I'm tutoring a student.   I'm taking tennis lessons.   I'm not studying every night!

B **GROUP WORK** Put your papers on the table. Take one paper and read the sentences. Your group guesses the name. Take turns.

A: This person is tutoring a student.

B: Is it Juliana?

C: No, it's not me!

D: Is it Kate?

C **GROUP WORK** Discuss the activities you're doing these days. Ask and answer questions for more information.

A: Who are you tutoring these days, Ken?

B: I'm tutoring a friend of mine. His name is Luke.

C: Are you tutoring him in English?

B: No, I'm not. I'm tutoring him in Japanese.

Picture story

A PAIR WORK Look at the pictures of David and Emma Salas. What did they do last weekend? Use the verbs to discuss your ideas.

clean	fix	play	stay out	watch
dance	paint	shop for	study	

A: David and Emma cleaned the house.

B: Emma fixed her bike.

B PAIR WORK Cover the pictures. What did David and Emma do last weekend? Answer with the information you remember.

Keep talking!

Memories

GROUP WORK Make five true sentences about your past activities with the phrases below. Your group asks three questions about each sentence for more information. Take turns.

Yesterday	Last night	Last weekend	Last month	Last year
I drank …	I ate …	I saw …	I bought …	I went …
I got up …	I went to bed …	I had …	I read …	I met …
I did …	I slept …	I drove …	I made …	I took …

A: Last night, I ate soup for dinner.

B: Did you eat in a restaurant?

A: No, I didn't. I ate at home.

C: Did you make the soup?

A: No, I didn't. My son made it.

D: Did you … ?

School trips

A PAIR WORK Add three more questions about school or work trips to the list. Then interview your partner. Take notes.

1 What was your favorite school or work trip?
_____

2 How old were you?
_____

3 How was the trip?
_____

4 Was there anything bad about the trip?
_____

5 Did you take a bus there?
_____

6 Were you there all day?
_____

7 Did you buy anything?
_____

8 _____

9 _____

10 _____

B PAIR WORK Tell another classmate about your partner's answers.

"Michi's favorite school trip was to a cookie factory. She was ten years old. The trip was …"

Keep talking!

What a vacation!

A Look at the items from Adriana's vacation. Write five questions and answers about her vacation.

1. Where did Adriana go on vacation?
   New York City.

2. What kind of music did she hear?
   Jazz music.

B GROUP WORK Cover the picture. Ask your questions. How many correct answers did your group get?

This weekend

A Make eight true sentences about your plans with the phrases below.

My plans		
I'm going to I'm not going to	dress up eat out go to a concert go to bed late go to the mall go window-shopping hang out study watch a movie work	tonight this evening tomorrow this weekend next Monday next Friday

dress up

go to a concert

go window-shopping

B **PAIR WORK** Tell your partner about your plans. Ask and answer questions for more information.

A: I'm going to go to bed late tonight.

B: Are you going to watch a movie tonight?

A: No, I'm not. I'm going to study.

Keep talking!

Party planners

A **GROUP WORK** Plan an end-of-class party. Take notes.

Date of party	Time of party	Place of party

Food and drink	Decorations	Music

A: When are we going to have our party?

B: Let's have it after class on Friday at 8:00.

C: OK. Now, where are we going to have it?

D: Let's have it here at the school.

B **CLASS ACTIVITY** Share your ideas. Ask and answer questions for more information.

A: We're going to have our party on Friday at 8:00.

B: It's going to be here at our school.

C: Which room is the party going to be in?

C **CLASS ACTIVITY** Vote for your favorite plan.

Irregular verbs

Base form	Simple past
be	was, were
become	became
build	built
buy	bought
can	could
choose	chose
come	came
do	did
draw	drew
drink	drank
drive	drove
eat	ate
fall	fell
feel	felt
fly	flew
get	got
give	gave
go	went
hang	hung
have	had
hear	heard
hold	held
know	knew
leave	left

Base form	Simple past
lose	lost
make	made
meet	met
pay	paid
read	read
ride	rode
run	ran
say	said
see	saw
sell	sold
send	sent
sing	sang
sit	sat
sleep	slept
speak	spoke
spend	spent
stand	stood
swim	swam
take	took
teach	taught
think	thought
wear	wore
win	won
write	wrote

Answer Key

Unit 9 Lesson A (page 144)
Keep Talking! Neighbors

Credits

The authors and publishers acknowledge the following sources of copyright material and are grateful for the permissions granted. While every effort has been made, it has not always been possible to identify the sources of all the material used, or to trace all copyright holders. If any omissions are brought to our notice, we will be happy to include the appropriate acknowledgements on reprinting and in the next update to the digital edition, as applicable.

Photography

All below images are sourced from Getty Images.

U1: Dougal Waters/DigitalVision; Nattakorn Maneerat/iStock/Getty Images Plus; drbimages/E+; mathiaswilson/E+; Alys Tomlinson/Cultura; kali9/E+; Gary John Norman/Blend Images; Vincent Sandoval/Getty Images Entertainment; Michael Tran/FilmMagic; Jason Merritt/Getty Images Entertainment; Kevin Winter/WireImage; Noam Galai/FilmMagic; PeopleImages/DigitalVision; ©Christa Van Den Heuvel; Jason Merritt/Getty Images Entertainment; Manuel Blondeau - Corbis/AOP Press/Corbis Sport; ©GV Cruz; Jim Spellman/WireImage; VCG/Visual China Group; ©Scott Gries; Kevin Mazur/WireImage; Victor Chavez/WireImage; Focus on Sport; Jason Merritt/TERM/Getty Images Entertainment; ©Jon Kopaloff; Ryan Pierse/Getty Images Entertainment; **U2:** miniature/DigitalVision Vectors; Marcus Chung /E+; ©Patricio Robles Gil; Caiaimage/Tom Merton/OJO+; JohnnyGreig/E+; Ronnie Kaufman/Larry Hirshowitz/Blend Images; Sami Sert/E+; Geber86/Vetta; Rob Lewine; PhotoAlto/Frederic Cirou/PhotoAlto Agency RF Collections; manaemedia/iStock/Getty Images Plus; ake1150sb/iStock/Getty Images Plus; **U3:** SeanShot/E+; Chris Craymer Limited/Stockbyte; H. Armstrong Roberts/ClassicStock/Archive Photos; Tom Kelley Archive/Retrofile RF; BeholdingEye/iStock/Getty Images Plus; koya79/iStock/Getty Images Plus; ©iStock; MihailDechev/iStock/Getty Images Plus; ©Hemera; ©E+; SKYRENDER/iStock/Getty Images Plus; Sean Justice/Photonica; gielmichal/iStock/Getty Images Plus; Cartarium/iStock/Getty Images Plus; Jerome Gorin/PhotoAlto; nipastock/iStock/Getty Images Plus; Yagi Studio/DigitalVision; maroke/iStock/Getty Images Plus; NYS444/iStock/Getty Images Plus; Eri Morita/Photodisc; Franco Origlia/Getty Images Entertainment; Images Plus; Dorling Kindersley; istock; Nikolai Sorokin; E+; ©istock; ©caimacanul/iStock/Getty Images Plus; Imagesource; creativesunday2016/iStock/Getty Images Plus; ©istock; Aire images/Moment; **U4:** Radius Images/Radius Images/Getty Images Plus; Light Thru My Lens Photography/Moment; Brent Winebrenner/Lonely Planet Images; artpipi/iStock/Getty Images Plus; microgen/iStock/Getty Images Plus; Uwe Krejci/DigitalVision; Karl Weatherly/Corbis Documentary; Education Images/Universal Images Group; miljko/E+; Fuse/Corbis; Sam Edwards/Caiaimage; Wavebreakmedia/iStock; Indeed; PeopleImages/E+; ©photodisc; ©Hero Images; ©Hemera; ©Istock; Yongyuan Dai/Stone; **U5:** iPandastudio/iStock/Getty Images Plus; monkeybusinessimages/iStock/Getty Images Plus; pictafolio/iStock/Getty Images Plus; OnstOn/iStock/Getty Images Plus; KeremYucel/iStock/Getty Images Plus; Jane_Kelly/iStock/Getty Images Plus; Madmaxer/iStock/Getty Images Plus; Geert Weggen/Aurora Photos; Westend61; JGI/Jamie Grill/Blend Images; Tetra Images; Photoplotnikov/iStock; MicrovOne/iStock; Jupiterimages/Photolibrary; Creative Crop/DigitalVision; Grzegorz Wozniak/EyeEm; rasslava/iStock/Getty Images Plus; UmbertoPantalone/iStock/Getty Images Plus; mattjeacock/iStock/Getty Images Plus; 3alexd/iStock/Getty Images Plus; valentinrussanov/E+; Morsa Images/Iconica; Boogich/E+; Ed Freeman/Stone; Danny Lehman/The Image Bank; Sam Edwards/OJO Images; golibo/iStock/Getty Images Plus; imagedepotpro/E+; ultramarinfoto/E+; Jeffrey Coolidge/Photodisc; Thomas-Soellner/iStock/Getty Images Plus; Spencer Platt/Getty Images News; Vimvertigo/iStock/Getty Images Plus; imtmphoto/iStock/Getty Images Plus; kali9/E+; Mint Images/Mint Images RF; Max shen/Moment; Westend61; Thearon W. Henderson/Getty Images Sport; Akimasa Harada/Moment Open; Tara Moore/DigitalVision; dlerick/iStock; **U6:** JohnnyGreig/E+; RUBEN RAMOS/iStock Editorial/Getty Images Plus; Digital Vision; PeopleImages/E+; ljubaphoto/iStock/Getty Images Plus; Andersen Ross/Cultura; Jenny Acheson/Stockbyte; Jupiterimages/The Image Bank; hjalmeida/iStock/Getty Images Plus; Wavebreak Media Ltd/Getty Images Plus; DAJ; Simon Potter/Image Source; Sven Hansche/EyeEm; LIU JIN/AFP; Steve Mason/Photodisc; PRImageFactory/iStock/Getty Images Plus; EricLatt/iStock Editorial; Owen Franken/Photolibrary; **U7:** ahirao_photo/iStock/Getty Images Plus; twomeows/Moment; Angela Schintu/EyeEm; zoranm/iStock/Getty Images Plus; Yulia_Kotina/iStock/Getty Images Plus; Jason England/EyeEm; MARIAMARTAGIMENEZ/iStock/Getty Images Plus; ©istock; ©E+/Getty Images; Wavebreakmedia/iStock/Getty Images Plus; MIXA; EricVega/iStock/Getty Images Plus; ©Hemera; Eric Audras/ONOKY; guruXOOX/iStock/Getty Images Plus; yulkapopkova/iStock/Getty Images Plus; Stockbyte; Zakharova_Natalia/iStock/Getty Images Plus; Photodisc; asbe/iStock/Getty Images Plus; Piotr Krzeslak/iStock/Getty Images Plus; rez-art/iStock/Getty Images Plus; ©Image Source; Claudia Totir/Moment; Maren Caruso/DigitalVision; SUNGSU HAN/iStock/Getty Images Plus; MargoeEdwards/iStock/Getty Images Plus; PhotoAlto/Laurence Mouton/PhotoAlto Agency RF Collections; Jupiterimages/PHOTOS.com/Getty Images Plus; Kevin Mazur/WireImage; **U8:** Willie B. Thomas/DigitalVision; guruXOOX/iStock/Getty Images Plus; ale_flamy/Moment; Jeff Greenberg/Universal Images Group; John Eder/Stone; zamrznutitonovi/iStock/Getty Images Plus; Alija/E+; csfotoimages/iStock Editorial/Getty Images Plus; Barry Winiker/The Image Bank; Joe McBride/The Image Bank; Fuse/Corbis; fotog; Wolfgang Kaehler/LightRocket; Josiah Edbrooke/iStock/Getty Images Plus; Tim Bieber/Photodisc; John Leyba/The Denver Post; John Leyba/The Denver Post; Chad Baker/Jason Reed/Ryan McVay/Photodisc; EThamPhoto/The Image Bank; DragonImages/iStock/Getty Images Plus; PhotoTalk/iStock/Getty Images Plus; andipantz/E+; Barry Winiker/The Image Bank; Alex Potemkin/E+; Thomas Barwick/Taxi; PRImageFactory/iStock/Getty Images Plus; PhotoAlto/Laurence Mouton/Getty Images Plus; **U9:** Westend61; Chris Whitehead/Image Source; SolStock/E+; Stadtratte/iStock/Getty Images Plus; microgen/iStock/Getty Images Plus; jacoblund/iStock/Getty Images Plus; Robert Deutschman/Robert Deutschman; Wavebreakmedia/iStock/Getty Images Plus; Tom Merton/Caiaimage; Wavebreakmedia/iStock; SeventyFour/iStock/Getty Images Plus; Alija/E+; Eric Audras/ONOKY; PeopleImages/E+; JGI/Tom Grill/Blend Images; fizkes/iStock/Getty Images Plus; Image Source/Getty Images; Dougal Waters/

DigitalVision; monkeybusinessimages/iStock/Getty Images Plus; drbimages/E+; schlol/E+; Qvasimodo/iStock/Getty Images Plus; John Harper/Stone; Parichat Boon-Ek/EyeEm; Peter Bannan/Moment; VStock LLC/Tanya Constantine; Mr.nutnuchit Phutsawagung/EyeEm; Ryan McVay/The Image Bank; Caiaimage/Paul Bradbury; Jose Luis Pelaez Inc/MNPhotoStudios/Blend Images; **U10:** Andreas Kuehn/DigitalVision; Klaus Vedfelt/DigitalVision; Andrea Pistolesi/Stone; Hoxton/Tom Merton/Hoxton; Photos.com/PhotoObjects.net; lewkmiller/iStock/Getty Images Plus; Wavebreakmedia/iStock/Getty Images Plus; Elke Meitzel/Cultura; Greg Hinsdale/The Image Bank; Thomas Barwick/Stone; Ryan McVay/The Image Bank; Huntstock/Getty Images; Harold M. Lambert/Archive Photos; DMEPhotography/iStock/Getty Images Plus; Aneese/iStock Editorial/Getty Images Plus; Andrew Olney/Getty Images; jarenwicklund/iStock/Getty Images Plus; bowdenimages/iStock/Getty Images Plus; MGP; Gregory Costanzo/; flashfilm/The Image Bank; Stockbyte/; Plume Creative; FluxFactory/E+; Erik Isakson/Blend Images/Getty Images Plus; BLOOMimage; **U11:** Jupiterimages/Stockbyte PhotoAlto/Ale Ventura/PhotoAlto Agency RF Collections; andresr/iStock/Getty Images Plus; PRImageFactory/iStock/Getty Images Plus; Caiaimage/Paul Bradbury; BLOOMimage; Andrey Danilovich/iStock/Getty Images Plus; Ascent Xmedia/Stone; Mark Gibson/Corbis Documentary; Glowimages; Lya_Cattel/iStock; JeanUrsula/E+; Image Source; robbie jack/Corbis Entertainment; istock/Getty Images; MangoStar_Studio/iStock/Getty Images Plus; andrej_k/iStock/Getty Images Plus; Manuel-F-O/iStock/Getty Images Plus; Andersen Ross/Blend Images; Ricky John Molloy/Photodisc; Javier Vicencio/Moment Unreleased; visualspace/iStock/Getty Images Plus; Westend61; Hector Vivas/Jam Media/LatinContent Editorial; MaRabelo/iStock/Getty Images Plus; Ferdaus Shamim/WireImage; Image Source; Ariel Skelley/DigitalVision; Oleh_Slobodeniuk/E+; theasis/iStock/Getty Images Plus; PhotoAlto/Ale Ventura/PhotoAlto Agency RF Collections; **U12:** Sam Edwards/OJO Images; Burke/Triolo Productions/The Image Bank; Stephanie Keith/Getty Images News; xavierarnau/E+; Jose Luis Pelaez Inc/Blend Images; Oliver Furrer/Stone; Shalom Rufeisen/500px/500Px; PhotoAlto/Laurence Mouton/Getty Images; Jose Luis Pelaez Inc/MNPhotoStudios/Blend Images; Westend61; GemaBlanton/iStock/Getty Images Plus; ArtMarie/E+; PhotoAlto/Ale Ventura/PhotoAlto Agency RF Collections; fotografixx/iStock/Getty Images Plus; Photo and Co/The Image Bank; Zorica Nastasic/E+; Brothers91/E+; Michael Powell/Photolibrary/Getty Images; YOSHIKAZU TSUNO/AFP; kali9/iStock; Ann Ronan Pictures/Print Collector/Hulton Archive; **End Matter:** VisionsofAmerica/Joe Sohm/Photodisc; Jeffrey Greenberg/Universal Images Group; Freelance MD-based photographer/Moment Open; hedgehog94/iStock/Getty Images Plus; -M-I-S-H-A-/iStock/Getty Images Plus; JerryPDX/iStock/Getty Images Plus; Radius Images/Getty Images Plus; pop_jop/DigitalVision Vectors; 4x6/iStock/Getty Images Plus; RichLegg/iStock/Getty Images Plus; baona/iStock/Getty Images Plus; alikemalkarasu/E+; Hemera Technologies/PhotoObjects.net/Getty Images Plus; Rawpixel/iStock/Getty Images Plus; ©Daniel Grill/Tetra; ©E+; ©imagesource; ©Tetra Images; ©istock; ©Greg Elms/StockFood Creative; ©PhotoAlto; ©Stockbyte; anna1311/iStock/Getty Images Plus; nicmifsud/iStock; McIninch/iStock/Getty Images Plus; vgajic/E+; Mikael Vaisanen/The Image Bank; iPandastudio/iStock/Getty Images Plus; Jonathan Knowles/Stone; Wavebreakmedia/iStock/Getty Images Plus; Clerkenwell/Vetta; kali9/E+; Image Source RF/DreamPictures; stockinasia/iStock Editorial; JGI/Jamie Grill/Blend Images; PeopleImages/E+; fotosipsak/iStock/Getty Images Plus; Hero Images.

Front Cover by Sergio Mendoza Hochmann/Moment; Betsie Van der Meer/DigitalVision; andresr/E+.
Back Cover by Monty Rakusen/Cultura.
The following images are sourced from other libraries:
U2: ©Joana Lopes/Shutterstock; ©RubberBall/Alamy; ©Derek Trask/Alamy; **U3:** ©Media Bakery; ©Shutterstock; Frank Veronsky; Oleksiy Maksymenko/Alamy; Squared Studios/Ocean/Corbis; ©slon1971/Shutterstock; **U4:** © Frank Veronsky; Shutterstock; Media Bakery; Pushish Images/Shutterstock; **U5:** © Frank Veronsky; ©Alex Segre/Alamy; **U6:** ©Golden Pixels/Alamy; ©Pinnacle Pictures/Media Bakery; **U7:** ©Evlakhov Valeriy/Shutterstock; ©Adrianna Williams/Corbis; ©Frank Veronsky; ©ampFotoStudio/Shutterstock; **U8:** Frank Veronsky; **U9:** Blend Images/Alamy; Ted Foxx/Alamy; **U11:** Idealink Photography/Alamy; tomas del amo/Alamy; Frank Veronsky; Ditty_about_summer/Shutterstock; IM_photo/Shutterstock; Neale Cousland/Shutterstock; **U12:** Frank Veronsky; **End Matter:** ©Judith Collins/Alamy; ©Hugh Threlfall/Alamy; ©Holger Burmeister/Alamy.

Illustration

Front Matter: Kim Johnson; John Goodwin; **U1:** Kim Johnson; QBS Learning; **U2:** Peter Ellis; QBS Learning; Dani Geremia/Beehive Illustration; **U3:** Dani Geremia/Beehive Illustration; Peter Ellis; Rob Schuster; Kim Johnson; QBS Learning; **U4:** QBS Learning; **U6:** Dani Geremia/Beehive Illustration; QBS Learning; **U8:** QBS Learning; **U9:** Szilvia Szakall/Beehive Illustration; Garry Parsons; Peter Ellis; QBS Learning; **U10–12:** QBS Learning; **End Matter:** Dani Geremia/Beehive Illustration; QBS Learning.

Dani Geremia/Beehive Illustration pp20, 26, 56, 129, 137; Szilvia Szakall/Beehive Illustration pp86, QBS Learning pp5, 16, 29, 30, 32, 33, 35, 40, 57, 59, 60, 76, 78, 79, 81, 93, 96, 99, 109, 120, 125, 126, 127, 130, 131, 132, 135,138, 141, 142, 143, 144, 146, 147, 149

Art direction, book design, and layout services: QBS Learning
Audio production: CityVox, NYC and John Marshall Media
Video production: Steadman Productions